Praise for *You've Got This*

"This book is a lifeline for new teachers—uplifting, practical, and full of heart. Suzanne Dailey and Rob Dunlop draw from real experience to support not just the teacher's practice, but the teacher's spirit. Their wisdom honors the emotional complexities of this work and lights a path through the early years with clarity and hope. Every new educator deserves this book. It is an encouraging, insightful companion for anyone starting in education."

—**Jim Knight**, founder and senior partner of Instructional Coaching Group

"Blending science-backed strategies with real-world wisdom from the classroom, this book helps new teachers develop confidence, emotional resilience, and sustainable habits from the start. This isn't about surviving your first year. It's about laying the foundation for a career filled with energy, impact, and joy."

—**Shawn Achor**, *New York Times* bestselling author of *The Happiness Advantage* and *The Power of Beliefs*

"*You've Got This* is a clear, empathetic, and research-informed resource for educators in their early years of teaching. Suzanne Dailey and Rob Dunlop combine practical guidance with deep respect for the emotional and professional realities of the work. They are two of the most genuine and authentic educators I know, and that authenticity makes this book both credible and comforting."

—**Tom Schimmer**, education author, speaker, and consultant

"Teaching in your first years can feel overwhelming, isolating, and nonstop. *You've Got This* meets new teachers where they are, offering practical guidance without losing sight of their humanity. Dailey and Dunlop normalize the challenges while helping educators build habits that support both effective teaching and personal well-being. This is the kind of book every new teacher should have within arm's reach so that they feel seen, supported, and better prepared in their work!"

—**Thomas C. Murray**, bestselling author and speaker

"Thoughtfully organized by the seasons of the school year, this book anticipates the questions and concerns new teachers are likely to have and offers practical advice. The experienced authors acknowledge both the challenges and the excitement of a new teacher's first year in the classroom."

—**Monica Burns**, EdD, author of *EdTech Essentials*

"This book is an essential read for new teachers. It offers a rare blend of research-based insight and practical, classroom-ready guidance for those entering the profession. Filled with clear, actionable strategies, it supports both professional success and personal well-being. *You've Got This* is a trusted companion that teachers will return to often as they navigate the challenges and joys of their careers."

—**Frank Purcaro**, assistant superintendent, Newtown (CT) Public Schools

"New teachers enter this demanding profession with passion, heart, and a desire to inspire the next generation of learners. Rob Dunlop and Suzanne Dailey combine trusted experience and insight to help educators thrive and sustain joy in their work. Readers will find inspirational quotes and practical advice to guide them with confidence from the start."

—**Ken Ehrmann**, elementary principal, Pennridge (PA) School District, and creator and host of *powerED Up* Podcast

"After years of supporting new teachers, I believe this book should be required reading in every teacher education program. Organized around the realities of the first year, it offers practical, timely advice and constant encouragement. It feels like having Rob and Suzanne beside you—guiding, reassuring, and empowering you when you need it most."

—**Kelly Diiorio**, retired principal and head of New Teacher Induction Program

"Every beginning teacher should be given this book to read and then revisit each term. Something new resonates every time. It is a clear, research-based, no-nonsense companion. Chapter 6 is a standout and covers content often missed in preservice and in-service PD. Don't skip it!"

—**Dorothy Buchanan**, former educator and coordinator of professional learning for teacher candidates, Brock University

YOU'VE GOT THIS

Also by Suzanne Dailey

Teach Happier This School Year:
40 Weeks of Inspiration and Reflection

Small Shifts to Teach Happier
(QuickWins! Strategy Cards)

SUZANNE DAILEY | ROBERT DUNLOP

YOU'VE GOT THIS

Finding Happiness and Success in Your First Years of Teaching

iste+ascd
Arlington, Virginia USA

iste+ascd™

2111 Wilson Boulevard, Suite 300 • Arlington, VA 22201 USA
Phone: 800-933-2723 or 703-578-9600
Website: iste-ascd.org • Email: memsupport@iste-ascd.org
Author guidelines: ascd.org/write

Richard Culatta, *Chief Executive Officer;* Genny Ostertag, *Managing Director, Book Acquisitions & Editing;* Susan Hills, *Senior Acquisitions Editor;* Mary Beth Nielsen, *Director, Book Editing & Design;* Miriam Calderone, *Senior Editor;* Lisa Hill, *Graphic Designer;* Cynthia Stock, *Typesetter;* Emily Reed, *Senior Director, Publishing Operations;* Kelly Marshall, *Production Manager;* Shajuan Martin, *E-Publishing Specialist*

PAPERBACK ISBN: 978-1-4166-3439-3 ASCD product #126007 n4/26
PDF EBOOK ISBN: 978-1-4166-3440-9; see Books in Print for other formats.
Quantity discounts are available: email programteam@ascd.org or call 800-933-2723, ext. 5773, or 703-575-5773. For desk copies, go to www.ascd.org/deskcopy.

Library of Congress Cataloging-in-Publication Data is available for this title.
Library of Congress Control Number: 2025054009

35 34 33 32 31 30 29 28 27 26 1 2 3 4 5 6 7 8 9 10 11 12

To those entering this profession,

thank you for answering the call to teach.

YOU'VE
GOT
THIS

An Opening Letter from Suzanne and Rob

Dear Reader,

Thank you for choosing this book as a companion as you navigate your first few years in education. Our goal is to provide you with some tried-and-true strategies and questions to consider as you begin this rewarding, worthwhile career. Throughout the book, we will often remind you that although teaching is one of the most challenging professions, it is also the best job in the world. You have the opportunity to be a "trajectory changer" for the hundreds (or thousands!) of students you will interact with over the years.

Like all careers, teaching includes both joyful aspects that continually reconnect you with your purpose and challenging aspects that may make you momentarily question your decision to become an educator. As you approach your first few years, we will work together to reinforce the reason you chose teaching. Toward the end of your career, you'll look back and want do-overs, but you'll also be proud of what you've accomplished and the permanent, positive impact you've had on students.

One of the reasons we are reliable supporters is our experience: We have each taught for 23 years, and during the last 13 years, we have worked closely with orientation and induction programs for new teachers. Together, we have helped more than 2,500 new teachers navigate their first three years teaching in Canada (Rob) and the United States (Suzanne). As we worked with new colleagues in their first years, we noticed some common challenges that they all faced regardless of grade level. We have compiled the strategies, advice, and reflection questions in this book not only to help you avoid unnecessary false starts, frustrations, and disappointments, but also to celebrate the inevitable successes you will encounter. Everything we share is meant to increase your comfort and confidence as you begin the important work of teaching.

You may be thinking, "I'm as ready as I'll ever be. I've taken the courses, I've done student teaching, I am totally ready for this." This may all be true. But there will also be times when you think, "We didn't learn about this in class! How am I expected to handle this?!" Our goal is to honor both reactions by providing an experienced perspective and advice for navigating common scenarios. We also want to normalize the emotions you feel (spoiler alert: It's normal to feel *everything* the first year!), so we've organized this book to follow you through the seasons of a school year, addressing the issues you are likely to face and connecting to the emotions you will likely feel at these specific times. Whether you need advice on preparing for your students to arrive, establishing systems and structures, sustaining momentum, or strengthening your craft, you will find proven strategies here that we have successfully used in our own careers.

Each chapter in this book includes a checklist that you can use as much or as little as you want. The checklist has two sections: one focused on the *happiness and success of your classroom* and the other on *your personal happiness and success*. Teacher well-being heavily influences student success; when you are able to show up and take care of yourself, you are better able to show up and take care of your students. Yes, all educators are here for their students. But we also must have the capacity to show up for ourselves, our families, our friends, and the causes we care deeply about outside school. We promise to honor both your personal lives and your professional lives throughout this book.

Many studies conducted by positive psychologists and social scientists have helped us better understand the many benefits, personal *and* professional, of being in a healthy headspace or heartspace, and this book will explore them in detail. If it's true that success brings happiness, it's also true that when we feel steady, grounded, aligned, and balanced, we are better able to discern the next right thing to do. Students also perform better when they have a happy, balanced teacher.

Congratulations on beginning this journey in education. We are so thankful that we began our education journey years ago, thrilled to be even a small part of the first few years of yours, and honored to help uncover what you can do to proactively support your happiness and success as a teacher. As they say, "The journey is better together."

Take a deep breath. You've got this!

All the best,
Suzanne and Rob

CHAPTER

Before the Students Arrive: Reconnecting to Your Purpose and Laying the Groundwork for Happiness and Success

Before tackling the *what* and the *how* of being a teacher, consider your *why*. Why did you decide to become an educator? This might be the most important question you ask yourself throughout your career—and one you may find yourself returning to again and again. The answer to this question has the potential to guide you, motivate you, and pick you up when you are down. It will also play a key role in helping you find more happiness and success as you grow as a teacher.

Think back to the first time you remember wanting to pursue a career in education. What was it about the profession that interested you? There must have been something that made you think, "I could see myself becoming a teacher!" From that point on, you made decision after decision that eventually led you to where you are right now: reading this book for new teachers!

The goal of this chapter is to help you clearly define your *why* as an educator before students walk into your classroom. This will help anchor you on the good days, the challenging days, and all the days in between. To begin, reflect on any experiences you had as a student that contributed to you becoming a teacher. Here are some questions to get you started:

- What do you remember most about your experience in elementary school?
- How did teachers contribute to your desire to be an educator?
- Do any teachers stand out in your memory? If so, what is it that makes them stand out?
- How did your experiences as a student change as you moved through middle school and high school?
- Did you have any experiences during your postsecondary education that piqued your interest in teaching?
- If teaching is a second career for you, what made you want to become a teacher?

Life experiences lead many of us into this profession. For some, the catalyst might be growing up in a family of teachers and wanting to follow in their footsteps; for others, it might be an "aha" moment they have in college. Regardless of what it is, there is a reason you became a teacher. Do your best to hold on to this reason tightly as you move throughout your career, as it will help keep you close to your purpose and rediscover your joy in challenging times.

Lead with Your *Why*

In a famous TED Talk from 2009, Simon Sinek presents the relationship between our *why*, *how*, and *what* as a "golden circle," with the *why* at the center driving the *how* and the *what* (see Figure 1.1). Here's how Sinek explains it:

> Every single person, every single organization on the planet knows what they do, 100 percent. Some know how they do it. . . . But very, very few people or organizations know why they do what they do. . . . By "why," I mean: What's your purpose? What's your cause? What's your belief? Why does your organization exist? Why do you get out of bed in the morning? And why should anyone care? [When] the way we think, we act, the way we communicate is from the outside in, it's obvious. We go from the clearest thing to the fuzziest thing. But the inspired leaders and the inspired organizations . . . all think, act, and communicate from the inside out. (Sinek, 2009)

Here is a good example of leading with your *why*. Barry White Jr., a 5th grade teacher, was interviewed after going viral for giving students personalized handshakes as they entered the classroom each day. He said, "When

FIGURE 1.1 **The Golden Circle**

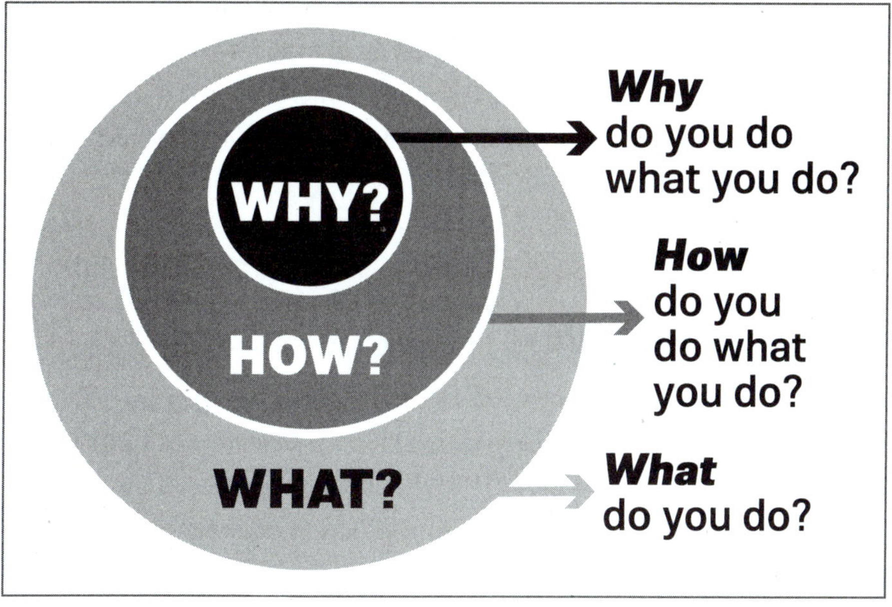

Source: Concept from *How Great Leaders Inspire Action* [Video], by S. Sinek, 2009, TED. https://www.ted.com/talks/simon_sinek_how_great_leaders_inspire_action

[students] come into school, I want this to be their sanctuary. . . . that's really why I do it, to bring joy to them" (WCNC.com, 2017). His *how* was building trust, making learning fun, and other ways of cultivating relationships with his students and getting them excited about school. The personalized handshakes were just one of many *whats* that this teacher had in place for his students.

It is easy to become overly focused on the *what* of being an educator: *what* teaching strategies will work best, *what* technology we are going to use, *what* assessment tools are most appropriate. These *whats* are very important and play a significant role in our students' success, but we should not focus on them so much that we lose sight of *why* we became teachers.

LESSONS LEARNED

Over the last six years, I have had the good fortune of helping to run a leadership program for teachers in our district. Many of the teachers who sign up are looking to reignite their passion as educators. One of the program's main

objectives is to reconnect these teachers to their *why*. On the last day, we sit in a circle and share what we think has been the most impactful part of the program. Participants' eyes will often well up with tears as they talk about finding their *why* again after having lost it somewhere along the way. Just by taking a moment to reconnect to their *why*, they feel more inspired and excited to go to work each day.

—Rob

Reflect on Your *Why*

As you prepare to enter your teaching career, take the time to reflect on your *why*. Most of us have a powerful reason for becoming a teacher. Try to capture this reason in a word or a phrase that you can carry with you throughout your career. Here are some examples of *why* statements used by teachers we have worked with:

- To be the caring adult to those who need me the most
- To inspire a love of learning
- To nurture the young minds of the next generation

Developing a *why* statement can be hard, and it is bound to be a work in progress. As you mature as an educator, take the time to reflect on your *why* statement and alter it as needed. The statement should keep you excited about making a difference in the lives of your students. Once you have developed a powerful *why* statement, post it somewhere you will see it multiple times a day: at the top your lesson plans, for example, or as a screensaver on your computer. Doing this ensures that you are reminded of your *why* daily and inspired to make it reality.

Take Lessons from the Blue Zones

Have you heard of the Blue Zones? These are regions of the world where people live longer and healthier lives than average. It is fascinating to learn about the factors that contribute to their longevity and high quality of life. (If you are looking for a great idea on which to base your geography lessons, the Blue Zones might be it!) As educators, we have to take care of ourselves before we can take care of others. It's worth looking to the Blue Zones for proven self-care strategies.

One leading researcher of the Blue Zones, Dan Buettner, identified the following lifestyle habits as contributing to the well-being of those who live in these regions. Consider how these might benefit you in your first years of teaching:

1. **Move naturally.** Incorporate movement into your day, such as by spending more time gardening or walking instead of driving to the store.
2. **Have a purpose.** Use your skills in ways that add meaning to your life and the lives of others.
3. **Downshift.** Add stress-relieving strategies to your daily routine.
4. **Stop eating once you're 80 percent full.** Avoid overeating—it just slows you down and makes you feel worse. Listen to your body when it tells you it is full.
5. **Eat a plant-based diet.** Try to eat more fruits, vegetables, and grains, as diets high in these foods can increase your life expectancy.
6. **Belong to a community.** Feeling connected to a community or something bigger than ourselves contributes to our health and well-being.
7. **Keep family and friends close.** Prioritize relationships with your family and close friends. Caring for your children and aging parents adds meaning to your life and can increase your life expectancy.
8. **Find the right tribe.** Ensure that your social circle supports healthy behaviors. (Buettner, 2017)

In this chapter, we want to focus on the second habit listed above: having a purpose. Living your life with a clear sense of purpose can positively affect your life in many different ways. For example, a 2019 study (Alimujiang et al., 2019) of more than 7,000 men and women found that having a purpose in life can lead to improved mental health and happiness, healthier lifestyle choices, stronger personal relationships, increased wealth, improved quality of life, and a longer lifespan. The more you research the benefits of having a purpose in life, the more important you realize it is.

Find Your Ikigai

One of the most interesting Blue Zones to learn about is the island of Okinawa, Japan. Many Okinawans have something they refer to as *ikigai*—their reason for being. García and Miralles (2017), authors of *Ikigai: The Japanese Secret to a Long and Happy Life*, conceptualized ikigai to reflect the intersection of four key overlapping elements: what we love, what the world needs, what we can be paid for, and what we are good at. To be fulfilled in our work, it is ideal to connect with all four of these elements.

As a profession, education meets at least two of the four requirements for ikigai easily: The world needs educators, and educators get paid to teach. But when it comes to "what we are good at" and "what we love," sometimes we need a little guidance.

Doing what we are good at. In our experience as educators, something that has always stood out to us is the sheer joy that new learning brings to educators. We have found that the teachers who are invested in their own professional learning and growth are also those who tend to be the most fulfilled and happy. The key is to embrace change and new learning as an opportunity to continually grow within the profession.

It takes time to get so good at teaching that it feels natural. There will be a lot to learn as a new teacher, and you should give yourself some grace by accepting that you do not need to learn it all in your first year. Just commit to improving one or two aspects of your teaching each year, and over time, you will build a program and skill set that you are proud of and that students respond to.

Doing what we love. If you can find a way to love coming to school each day, you will become the best version of yourself for your students. Try to always remember what you first loved about teaching and look for ways to create more experiences each day that bring you happiness and fulfillment.

It is important to make your happiness a priority. Happiness is a discipline that you need to work on over time. Throughout your career, you will need to invest time and energy in reconnecting with what you love about teaching and refocusing on what brings you joy in the profession. There will be seasons in your career when this is easier to do than others, but knowing that we have the agency to increase our happiness empowers us to make small, positive shifts in our thoughts, language, and actions regardless of the season.

Now that we have zoomed out to connect to our purpose and honor ourselves as human beings, let's zoom in on the classrooms and focus on the logistics of your first year.

Get to Know the People

In 2013, Jennifer Gonzalez wrote a blog post titled "Find Your Marigold" that went viral. In it, she shares how organic farmers often plant marigolds around the perimeter of their gardens to protect new crops against predators, providing optimal conditions for them to grow and flourish. In the same way, there are key individuals in your building who can serve as *your* marigolds, helping you grow and flourish in the upcoming school year by connecting you with people and resources, strengthening your skill set, and encouraging both your head and your heart.

Before your students arrive at school, it's important to start building essential relationships with your colleagues. We encourage you to be proactive and reach out to the people in the roles discussed in this section, as they will undoubtedly be among your many marigolds by the end of the school year.

Head Custodian

You've more than likely already spoken to the head custodian in your building as you've looked for your room and organized your space. Ask them how they prefer to communicate: Some folks don't mind being asked to do things while passing in the hallway, while others prefer an email. I often keep a sticky note of things to ask our custodian about before school begins. One of the questions I'm sure to ask is where they like to get coffee or lunch. A small gift card to express your appreciation goes a long way!

Building Secretary

The building secretary is the heart of any school. This person knows all the ins and outs, people and places, and rules and routines. It is essential that you connect with your building secretary so they can help you get what you need and provide you with important information before the year begins (e.g., when to submit attendance rolls, where to find supplies, whom to reach out to for missing curriculum materials). Your questions are important, so please ask them! At the same time, it's important to keep in mind that the building secretary is often multitasking for many people. Understanding their work rhythms and preferences will help you get what you need while honoring their needs as well.

School Nurse

School nurses are the wonderful people who keep our students healthy—and they are there for you, too! Find out where the nurse is located, when to send students to see them, and what they suggest you should keep in your room for emergencies. If you or your students have any medical needs, be sure you connect with your nurse ahead of time in the event you end up needing something during the school day.

Guidance Counselor

Your beloved guidance counselor has come to know your students really well over a long period of time. They can provide a valuable perspective on your incoming students' needs and their academic, social, and emotional journeys. They often have wonderful resources that can help you establish a positive classroom environment and teach social-emotional skills to your students.

Tech Support

If something technological isn't working in your classroom, your school or district tech support is invaluable. Find out if you have someone on staff full time in this role and whether they serve just your school or multiple buildings. Ask them what the process is for requesting help when you need it. (Some districts use a help-ticket system, while others communicate through email or other avenues.) Make sure to connect with tech support before students first enter your classroom so that you can feel confident using educational technology with them.

Everybody Else's Marigold

Most schools have that one person who seems to be everyone's go-to for just about all things. Keep an ear out for hints like, "That's a good question, let me ask Elise" or "I bet Elise has a [insert unique item such as a brass fastener, pipe cleaner, extra beaker]" or "You know who would know that? Elise." Whoever your school's Elise is, find them and hold them close at the start of the year. They are sure to be your marigold too by year's end!

"Your" Person

Be on the lookout for someone you think could be a good source of support this year. This person should be able to help you professionally and make you feel good at work. This is someone you may even want to spend time with outside school. Keep your eyes open for that colleague who models a healthy perspective, has a good sense of humor, and honors a work-life balance.

LESSONS LEARNED

One of my most beloved colleagues is Elise, a kindergarten teacher who has been teaching for *55 years* and is still one of the most energetic, loving, innovative teachers in the district! I continue to go to Elise for insight and help. If I've got a question about the school's history or journey, Elise knows the answer. If I need to know more about a specific family, Elise has dealt with them and can provide a helpful perspective.

—Suzanne

Create an Inviting, Student-Centered Classroom

We've all seen them: the Pinterest-perfect classrooms. There are themes, there are color schemes. Yes, they are lovely, and yes, you may want to copy/paste that classroom into yours. And there will be time for that—later. Right now, let's focus on some basic priorities.

Start Simple

It can be overwhelming to think about where to start when setting up your classroom, especially when you're staring at blank classroom walls and wondering how you will fill the space. Here's a statistic that should help you feel a little better: Studies show that visually cluttered walls can overwhelm students who are still developing their capacity to maintain focus and ignore distractions (Godwin et al., 2022). In other words, too much can be . . . well, too much. So give yourself permission to dial down the "decorative volume."

As author and happiness expert Gretchen Rubin (2019) reminds us, "Outer order contributes to inner calm" (p. 1). With this in mind, a good rule to follow is that about 20 to 40 percent of your wall space should be empty. A little decoration, some student work, and a few curricular resources that reinforce learning, such as anchor charts, are all you need on the walls. Strive for a balance of academic support, student work, and purposefully vacant spaces or splashes of color to promote a feeling of calm.

LESSONS LEARNED

One new teacher I know recently spent hundreds of dollars on a perfectly curated kit of borders, signs, letters, pom-poms, decorative lanterns—all of it. Her classroom looked like something out of a magazine. But when her students arrived in this picture-perfect space, there was no room for them to display their work. This teacher and I spent an evening after school taking down the decor and rearranging just about everything on the walls to make space for student work. When we were finished, the space had become a calmer and more collaborative, student-friendly space.

—Suzanne

Display Student Work

It's of utmost importance that students feel they belong in their classroom. Remember, this isn't just your classroom; it's theirs as well. The space belongs to everyone who learns within those walls. So consider how you will want to honor the work of your students in your classroom. To both acknowledge students' efforts and conserve your own energy, you may want to dedicate a specific space to student work on the walls with a banner like "Spotlight On. . . ." Some teachers go so far as to create a faux refrigerator door on which they post students' papers; others hang work on a simple clothesline with clothespins. Whatever works for you is great, as long as it allows for space to make students feel proud of their accomplishments. (Note: If you don't have room to showcase all your students' work at once, keep a running list of whose work has been posted so you can make sure nobody is left out and everyone's progress is acknowledged and celebrated.)

Add Lighting and Plants

Do you remember when you were a student and your teacher would show a movie? The lights would go off, the movie would start, and everyone would settle in. When the movie was over, the overhead lights would come on and students would reflexively shield their eyes. School lighting can sometimes feel harsh not only to our students, but to ourselves as well. Lighting plays a significant role in how we feel and how our minds focus, so it's important to consider this element when envisioning the physical layout of our classroom.

Some of us have dimmers on the light switches in our classrooms. It may sound silly, but these can be easy to miss. This happened in Suzanne's school district, where teachers in a school that had undergone a building renovation complained about the harsh lighting. What they hadn't realized was that the new light plates included a dimmer switch, which by default was set to the brightest level! Once the teachers discovered the dimmer, they were able to adjust the light in their classrooms to a brightness that suited both them and their students. (If you don't have a dimmer switch in your classroom, consider turning off every other switch or using lamps instead of the overhead light for a softer, calmer feel.)

If you have windows in your classroom, you are lucky: Research shows that students feel less stressed and more focused when natural light filters in from outside (Lindemann-Matthies et al., 2021). Adding a few indoor plants to the room is another way to bring a little of the outside in. Plants can also help absorb noise and purify the air in the room.

Provide Flexible Seating Options

Many school districts recognize that the physical environment plays a key role in student productivity. Before your students arrive, envision how you can create a versatile work environment for students with flexible seating options. A space that offers students choice empowers them to select the seating arrangement they find most comfortable and productive, whether that's a traditional desk, a standing desk, a couch, a balance ball chair, or something else. If you don't have many options to offer in your classroom, allow students flexibility in how they use what you do have and be sure to rearrange the classroom layout throughout the year. The more versatile the layout, the greater the opportunity to increase student comfort and engagement. (A word of caution: Classroom setups that work for your students one year may not work with next year's class—not because you're doing anything wrong, but simply because each group of kids has its own needs or preferences.)

Regularly asking students to provide feedback about your room's layout allows students to feel like it truly is a shared space. Invite your students to complete a classroom audit as a way to share how they feel about the classroom environment. Making adjustments based on their input helps students feel seen and heard. (See Chapter 3 for a more detailed discussion of classroom audits.)

When students truly feel like they belong in their learning environment, they are more likely to be engaged and regulated, and our jobs as teachers are more likely to be joyful.

Use Legible Fonts on Signs and Posters

Many themed packages exist specifically for teachers that include matching schedules, anchor charts, alphabets, and other resources for posting on the walls. These packages are intended to make a classroom look beautiful and cohesive when everything is displayed. If you are in the market for one of these packages, be sure to consider the font they use for letters—especially if your students are just learning how to read and write. It's more important for displays to be legible than it is for them to be especially eye-catching (see Figure 1.2). Prioritize clear, legible fonts that can support students' growth as emerging readers and writers. Displays that

FIGURE 1.2 **The Importance of Legible Fonts**

Example

Prioritize clear, legible fonts that can support students' growth as emerging readers and writers.

Nonexample

DISPLAYS THAT ARE DIFFICULT FOR STUDENTS TO DECODE ARE A WASTE OF MONEY AND REAL ESTATE THAT CAN FRUSTRATE STUDENTS AND ENCOURAGE THEM TO USE POOR DECODING STRATEGIES.

are difficult for students to decode are a waste of money and real estate that can frustrate students and encourage them to use poor decoding strategies.

Find Your Resources

You've connected with your building colleagues. You've considered the layout of the classroom. Now you are ready for the good stuff: teaching! As a newer teacher, it is of utmost importance that you teach the curriculum your district has hired you to teach. Before students arrive in your class, make sure to get answers to the following questions.

What resources am I expected to use? Are there specific books you are expected to use? Is software available to support curriculum implementation? What are the rules for supplementing district curriculum materials with materials of your own?

Where do I find the resources? You'll want to know where resources like books or manipulatives are located (e.g., library, book closet, someone else's classroom) so you can give yourself enough time to find them, review them, and plan appropriately for their use.

When do I use the resources? It may be overwhelming to see all the resources you are expected to teach. Ask if there is a pacing guide for the school year that maps out when to use them. Pacing guides help us stay on track and ensure that we give our students enough time to learn skills or concepts. Don't worry if your pace is a little slower than your more experienced colleagues'; that is very common. Just make sure you aren't weeks off from where they are. Consider aiming for a pace that keeps you two or three days behind your department or grade-level peers. That way, you can ask them what went well or what they would adjust before you tackle a lesson. Pacing in Year 1 may feel a little rocky, and that's OK. Give yourself some grace; you can always refine the pacing next year. In fact, it's always a good idea to leave notes on your lesson plans, reminding you to slow down here, speed up there, combine lessons, or spread lessons over multiple days. Your future self will be so thankful for these notes!

How can I access online resources? If you use digital resources that require login information, the first thing you want to know is if students have a single sign-on (SSO) to manage their passwords. If they don't, be sure you have any necessary usernames and passwords ahead of time. It's also important to find out whether students will need login credentials to access opportunities for additional practice or supplemental materials. For younger students who need multiple logins, consider giving each one a paint swatch with four to six colors on it that has a different login written out on each color.

Who can help me? If you are lucky enough to work in a district with people in dedicated positions to help implement curriculum effectively, it's your professional responsibility to call upon them. Instructional coaches, reading specialists, math and literacy coaches, program specialists, staff developers—all these individuals are literally paid to help you teach! Ask them questions, co-plan lessons with them, invite them to teach a lesson to your students, or ask them to watch you teach and provide nonevaluative feedback. This kind of targeted, job-embedded professional development can help hone your craft and increase your confidence while also strengthening collegial relationships with staff beyond your grade level, department, or building.

Figure Out Your Workflow

File this under "things you already know": Time is your most precious commodity. How can you maximize your productivity while creating engaging lessons for your students? Be mindful of how long it is taking you to design lessons and how much time you spend teaching them. As you start to put lesson plans into action in the first few weeks of school, periodically pause to reflect on what works for you in terms of planning, preparation, delivery, and reflection.

Warning: Don't Get Stuck in Your Slides!

Have you ever sat in a meeting or professional development session where the facilitator doesn't deviate from their slides? It's maddening, and students feel the same way. When we become overly reliant on slides, it can be hard to go off script and address student questions or take advantage of a teachable moment. Give yourself permission to monitor, adjust, and move away from your slides to further student learning.

Maximize Your Mentor

In Shawn Achor's 2018 book *Big Potential*, we learn about a study in which a person is asked to describe a steep mountain in front of them, first by themselves and then with a trusted colleague by their side. Guess what the study found? The second time the person described the mountain, they described it as 10–20 percent less steep than they had before—because, with a colleague next to them, they now felt supported.

Many districts have designated mentors in place to help you navigate the upcoming school year. To make a long story short: *Use them!* Mentors know the ins and outs of your district and school dynamics and have been chosen for their ability to help you learn them, too. Your mentor can help save you time, energy, and even your sanity.

We often see new teachers reluctant to ask questions because they "don't want to be a bother." You are not bothering your mentor by asking them questions! Remember, they were once in your shoes. This may surprise you, but many experienced teachers love answering questions; they see it as paying back the support that was once given to them.

LESSONS LEARNED

Every year, I hear the same thing from at least two or three mentors: "Suzanne, my mentee keeps saying she doesn't need my help and everything is fine, but it's not going well at all. How can I help her?" Mentors see it as a red flag when mentees report that everything is fine and they don't need anything. They know very well that in everybody's first year, very little is fine and a lot of help is needed!

—Suzanne

Find a time that works within the rhythms of your day to connect regularly with your mentor *and get it on the calendar*, especially if you don't share the same planning or prep time. If it's not on the calendar, it's less likely to happen! Try to meet with them before school, after school, or at lunch a couple of days each week. Making time to learn from an experienced colleague will save you time in the long run.

Here are just a few questions worth asking your mentor at the start of the school year:

- What are the contracted or expected times for teacher arrival and dismissal?
- What are the professional dress expectations?
- Can you show me different classroom setups?
- Would you please share your Day 1 or Week 1 plans?
- How often should I communicate with parents, and in what way?
- What are some "must-knows" for my first two weeks of teaching?
- What relationship-building activities do you have students do in the first week of school?
- When is Back to School Night? Can you share how you present during Back to School Night so I can adhere to expectations?
- Can you share some effective classroom management strategies? How do you positively acknowledge when the class or individual students engage in desired behaviors?
- What format are lesson plans expected to be in, and when and how should I submit them to the principal?
- Which individuals in the school or district should I prioritize knowing and connecting with?

LESSONS LEARNED

Luckily for me, my sister and I were teaching partners my first year back. She has been my mentor and a lifesaver. She knows me better than anyone and really helped me adjust to being back in the classroom after 11 years in different positions.

One piece of advice she gave me that made an incredible difference in my first month was that my students were just responding to the energy I was giving them. At the time, I was very stressed out about meeting every curriculum expectation and doing things perfectly. She reminded me to relax, which in turn led students to open up, allowing us to start building relationships. Now we are having a lot of fun together, and I enjoy going to work every day.

—Rob

As a new teacher, you have limited amounts of time and energy to dedicate to new professional relationships, so take advantage of opportunities that come up. For example, if you see colleagues packing up on a Friday and heading to happy hour, don't automatically think to yourself, "I can't go, I have so much to do." You will *always* "have so much to do." Log off, zip up your bag, and head out with your colleagues. We have found that time spent connecting with peers out of school strengthens your relationships with them, which can boost your productivity and happiness *in* school.

Connect with Students and Families Before the First Day

As parents, we've both experienced firsthand how impactful the first communication from your child's new teacher can be. Within moments of reading that initial email or letter, you form an impression of the person who will guide and care for your child over the next 10 months. Judgmental, we know, but it's the truth! A well-crafted, thoughtful, and informative message free of careless errors inspires confidence in you and optimism for the year ahead. By contrast, a letter lacking these qualities can quickly raise concerns.

The first message to parents is important for all teachers, but especially for those new to a school. An underwhelming communication from a veteran teacher who has built a solid reputation and strong connections within the school community might not raise concerns because they've got years of experience to back them. A new teacher has no such safety net. This is your chance to make a meaningful first impression, so put in the time and effort to craft a thoughtful, polished message that reassures families and gets them excited for the year ahead. You only get to make one first impression, so make it count!

Decide on a Format

Before you start composing your first communication to parents, do some research on what the norms are at your new school. People are creatures of habit, so go with whatever format parents are most familiar with.

There are benefits to any format you choose. Mass emails and text messages allow you to quickly send communications to everyone and be confident they make it home. They also let you link to class websites and online forms that you might want parents to complete. You're not limited by space, so you can share everything you need to without running out of room. On the other hand, a physical letter home created with an online template can be more visually appealing to the reader. When you choose your template, be sure to consider what it will look like in black and white (unless you are the rare teacher who has access to a color printer). Keep it simple: Aim for one page, front and back if necessary. And if you want to include links, create QR codes. They are easy to make and, in printed format, easier to use than URLs, and you will immediately impress parents with your tech skills while giving them something tangible to talk about at home.

Craft a Memorable First Communication

We highly recommend reviewing communications your colleagues plan to share with students and families before drafting your own. No need to reinvent the wheel! Then, when you are ready to begin drafting your first communication, consider including the following elements:

- **A warm greeting and excitement for the year.** Begin by expressing your enthusiasm for the upcoming year and your excitement about meeting your new students. A simple statement like "I am thrilled to be your child's teacher this year and can't wait to embark on this learning journey together" sets a positive tone.

- **A brief introduction.** Share a little about yourself, including your background, teaching experience, and philosophy. Highlight what makes you passionate about teaching and your goals for the classroom. For example, you might say, "I believe every child deserves a safe, inclusive environment where they can thrive and develop a love for learning."
- **Your vision for the classroom.** Outline the type of environment you plan to create, emphasizing inclusivity, respect, and collaboration. Let parents know you are committed to fostering a space where every child feels valued and supported.
- **Key information.** Include practical details, such as the names of other teachers or school personnel the student will interact with during the day, contact information for you and other relevant staff, and a list of items students will need for the first day (as well as a list of those that will be provided).
- **Digital resources.** If you have a classroom website or use digital tools like Google Classroom, provide a link or QR code. This gives families easy access to ongoing updates and resources.
- **Communication channels.** Share the best way for families to reach you and emphasize your openness to collaboration. A sentence such as "Please don't hesitate to contact me with any questions or concerns" reinforces your commitment to partnership.
- **Opportunities for parent input.** Parents like to know you are ready to partner with them during the school year. Consider saying something such as "If there is anything you would like me to know about your child before the first day of school, please email me." Even if parents don't end up contacting you, offering them the opportunity to share information about their child starts the year on a positive note.

Be sure to proofread your message thoroughly. Spelling and grammar mistakes can quickly undermine your professionalism. You can use tools like a spell checker or AI, or ask a colleague or mentor to review your message before sending it out. Read aloud what you've written so you can hear the tone and cadence. One strategy is to read your message backward, sentence by sentence, to check your grammar and keep the language fresh.

Finally, make sure your communication is visually appealing. Use a tool like Canva to create a professional layout with letterhead, images, or even a Bitmoji. A well-designed letter feels especially personal and engaging.

Remember That Timing Is Key

Before you send your communication, ask colleagues when they typically send theirs out. You'll want to ensure your timing aligns with school policies and communication protocols. Sending your letter too early or too late could result in confusion or missed opportunities to connect. (Note: Do not forget to review your social media or change your privacy settings before introducing yourself. Some parents will go straight to social media to find out more about you, so double-check that you are ready for that.)

Prepare for Back to School Night

Some schools will have a Back to School Night before the school year begins, while others will hold theirs within the first few weeks of school. Regardless of when such events are scheduled, they are wonderful opportunities to make another positive impression and connect with families. Here are some tips to ensure success:

- Be sure your classroom is welcoming, clean, and organized.
- Dress professionally.
- Have any handouts, resources, or activities ready to go.
- Rehearse your presentation ahead of time. It can be intimidating to speak in front of a room of adults!

If you decide to collect information from parents about their child, consider prompts such as these:

- How does your child feel about school [or the class subject]?
- What successes and challenges has your child experienced in school that you would like me to know about?
- Does your child have friends in this class? If so, please list them.
- What is something your child enjoys outside school?

You can also use this opportunity to confirm emails, phone numbers, and preferred ways of communication. Consider having parents engage in short activities like the following when they visit your classroom:

- Provide parents with index cards on which to write encouraging messages to their child. Alternatively, give parents a white crayon to write a quick greeting on an index card; the next day, have students use a colored crayon to color the card, revealing the "mystery message."
- Provide a selection of inspirational quotes on index cards for parents to choose from. On the back of the quote they choose, they can write a little note to their child.
- Provide parents with a template and a sentence starter (e.g., "I am proud of you because . . .") for a message to leave on their child's desk.

Remember, this is your chance to make a meaningful first impression with families before students walk through your classroom door. When you take the time to create thoughtful, polished communications, you are taking the first step to a successful school year.

Take Care of School-Year You

We can control only two things in our teaching role: how we *prepare*, and how we *respond*. You've done so much so far to prepare for your students: You've reconnected to your purpose, introduced yourself to building colleagues, created an inviting classroom space, located district resources, connected with families, and envisioned what the first day and week of school could look like. You are putting energy exactly where it needs to be, but we encourage you to also harness some energy for *yourself.*

The first day of school is nearing—and let us please normalize the back-to-school nightmares that every teacher gets, even after retirement! As most of your thoughts and energy are going into that important first day with students, we'd like you to keep in mind this saying: *Take care of people who take care of people*. In this new school year, you will be responsible for taking care of many people: your students. As you tirelessly prepare for them, we urge you to prepare for your own needs, too. We understand that the launch of a new school year can be a challenging time to prioritize school-year you—after all your classroom preparations, there isn't a lot of time, space, energy, or bandwidth left over for self-care—but please try to do these small but powerful things:

- **Stay hydrated.** Find a reusable water bottle that can keep water cold and sip from it throughout the day.
- **Fuel your body.** Good nutrition is important to keep your body and mind working at optimal levels. Do your best to reduce your intake of processed foods and pack salads, nuts, and other nutrient-dense foods.
- **Get some sleep.** Proper sleep is tremendously important at all times, but you need it now more than at any other time of the school year. A rested body and mind are necessary to make good decisions, maintain perspective, and have some energy left to do something after a busy school day.
- **Prepare beforehand.** Plan or pack your lunch the night before, set the coffee timer to go off in the morning, cut up fruits and vegetables so they are easy to grab as you walk out the door—these are just a few things you can do to make sure you're ready to go in the mornings.
- **Disconnect at night.** We recommend setting an alarm on your phone reminding you to disconnect and unwind at the end of the day.

CHAPTER 1 CHECKLIST

Hopefully this chapter has you thinking of ways you can prepare for the arrival of your students. As you check off the items below, you will feel more and more prepared for the weeks ahead. Make sure you don't forget to take care of *you* while you are preparing for your students!

Happiness and Success for Your Students and Classroom

- ☐ Connect with your marigolds:
  - ☐ Head custodian
  - ☐ Building secretary
  - ☐ School nurse
  - ☐ Guidance counselor
  - ☐ Tech support
  - ☐ Other
- ☐ Dedicate a space in the classroom for displaying student work.
- ☐ Locate the curriculum resources you need.
- ☐ Bring in simple decorations, plants, and lights to make your room feel welcoming.
- ☐ Figure out classroom seating arrangements.
- ☐ Find and use pacing guides.
- ☐ Ask your mentor questions about getting the school year started.
- ☐ Find out when and how you are expected to contact families.
- ☐ Write a welcoming message to parents and have it reviewed by a colleague.
- ☐ Send your welcoming letter out at the same time as your colleagues.
- ☐ Brainstorm ways to involve parents on Back to School Night.
- ☐ Make sure you have nothing objectionable on your social media accounts.

✓

Happiness and Success for You

- ☐ Define your *why* and make it visible.
- ☐ Draw an ikigai diagram with four overlapping circles featuring your four ikigai elements and post it in your classroom.
- ☐ Focus on relationship building with colleagues.
- ☐ Make time each day to downshift and practice self-care.
- ☐ Give yourself grace. You are new to this—be gentle on yourself.
- ☐ Meet up with a friend after work.
- ☐ Make sure you are getting enough sleep.
- ☐ Stay hydrated throughout the day.
- ☐ Plan and pack healthy snacks and lunch.
- ☐ Set a timer at night to signal when it's time to disconnect and rest.

✓

CHAPTER

The Students Are Here!
Creating the Conditions for Classroom Happiness and Success

Regardless of the grade level you teach, one thing is certain: You won't start the first week of school teaching curriculum content. Your lesson plans for Week 1 won't look like the ones for the rest of the year; they're more like a series of lists. Planning your first few weeks can feel messy and piecemeal, and that's totally normal. This period is an opportunity to set the tone, build relationships, and establish routines.

Build Connections with Students

Have you ever heard it said that teachers shouldn't smile for the first three weeks of school? We recommend the opposite. In fact, we say smile from the very first minute so students can feel as welcomed as possible. This is the first step to connecting with your students as both a loving, supportive adult *and* the authority figure in the room. It isn't a matter of being either kind or firm; you can, and should, be both. Read on to learn how you can strike an appropriate balance of authority and love in the classroom.

Greet Students at the Door

When your students walk into their classroom for the first time, one of the easiest ways to signal to them that they are seen and supported is to greet them at the door. According to Laura Mooiman (2023), research shows that greeting students at the door has the following benefits:

- A 20 percent increase in student engagement
- A 9 percent decrease in disruptive behavior
- An increased overall sense of belonging among students

In our own experience, greeting students at the door has almost always led to favorable outcomes. As an 8th grade teacher, Rob has multiple classes cycling in and out of his classroom all day. He has found that greeting students at the door and checking in with them as they arrive helps decrease the sense of chaos many students feel when changing classes. It is also an opportunity to make a quick connection before the learning begins.

LESSONS LEARNED

Because elementary students remain in the same classroom for most of the day, it's important for teachers to start their time together every day in as positive a way as possible. I try to always greet students as they walk into the classroom in the morning. I've found that on the days when I couldn't make it—due to an unexpected phone call, for example, or a meeting that ran late—behavioral issues tended to arise more frequently than they did when I was able to greet students at the door.

—Suzanne

Here are a few simple yet impactful greetings you can use to welcome students at the door:

- "I'm glad you're here."
- "I saw this [book/picture/reel] and thought of you."
- "Today is going to be a great day."
- "Did you get a new haircut?"

- I like your new shoes."
- "Did you watch [show or game] last night?"
- "I missed you yesterday. Are you feeling better?"
- "How was your [performance or game]?"
- "I was thinking of you yesterday. Did you tell your family about [anecdote or accomplishment from the day before]?"

Make a Positive First Impression

Your very first time together with students in the classroom should set the tone for the rest of the year. Start off by welcoming the students and relaying to them your excitement about being their teacher. Follow this up with a short overview of your goals for the year and a bit about yourself. It can be easy to "over-talk" in these initial interactions, so do your best to avoid talking for an extended period. Consider leading a fun icebreaker or other activity that will help you learn students' names and some information about them. (We offer a few concrete examples later in this chapter.) Prior to introducing an activity, share your expectations to ensure that it goes well—and when it *does* go well, praise your students! Positive reinforcement is the key to effective classroom management. Following are a few activities you can use in class to learn more about your students.

Biography Bag. This idea can be used with students of any age. Provide each student with a small paper bag. (If you'd like, you could ask them to personalize the bag by decorating it.) Then, ask them to bring in three to five objects that reflect something about themselves and place them in the bag. Over the next few days, provide time for students to share their objects with the class.

It is important to create your own bag ahead of time to share with the class. This is a good way to model expectations, give students ideas, and share a little bit about yourself. Here are a few examples of things you might place in your bag:

- A photo of your family
- A pet treat or toy if you have a pet at home
- Something related to a hobby (e.g., a book or a tennis ball)
- A postcard or photo of a place you've been to or want to visit

If you are teaching older students, you may ask them to include a notecard explaining their items. This increases the rigor of the assignment, provides students with support when sharing with the class, and gives you a glimpse into their writing.

Find Someone Who. This is a fun one that you can create a template for and reuse over the years. Have students fill in a simple grid (usually 3x3, 4x4, or 5x5) with their interests or hobbies. (If your students are younger, you can prefill the squares with common descriptors like those in the example in Figure 2.1.) Throughout the first week of school, occasionally pause some procedural or introductory instruction and create time for students to "find someone who" has done something included in their grid. As students circulate around the room to connect with one another, they put their initials in a box that applies to them. For example, if Emerson Jones's template has a box reading "has a dog" and Keegan Smith has a dog, then Keegan would write "KS" in that box. This is a nice way for students to move around and learn about their classmates while also giving you a glimpse into their lives.

"You Will Learn a Lot This Year," by A. Teacher. This back-to-school activity is a favorite of ours to help you kick off the year with kindness and authority. As the teacher, write an "article" that outlines some facts about yourself and what students will be doing in your class in the upcoming year. Figure 2.2 shows a condensed example of an article Suzanne wrote in

FIGURE 2.1 **"Find Someone Who . . ." Bingo Card**

B	I	N	G	O
Has traveled to more than three states	Has a pet	Likes to play outside	Collects something	Likes sports
Can speak a second language	Plays videogames	Likes to make crafts or art projects	Read a great book over the summer	Has a sibling
Likes to cook or bake	Can tell a joke that makes everyone laugh	FREE SPACE!	Has a hidden talent	Likes to play card games
Likes to play board games	Can play a musical instrument	Can juggle or perform a magic trick	Has flown on a plane	Likes to dance
Can name their favorite teacher	Likes to listen to music	Volunteers for a local charity or organization	Has lived in a different city for more than a year	Went to a sporting event this summer

FIGURE 2.2 **Example Teacher "Article"**

"You Will Be Very Busy This Year in 4th Grade"
by A. Teacher

You are going to be very busy this year in 4th grade!

Your teacher is Mrs. Dailey. She has always wanted to be a teacher and is very happy that this is her fourth year at Mill Creek. Before being a teacher at Mill Creek, Mrs. Dailey taught 4th grade in Rochester, New York, at the Fred Hill Elementary School and 5th grade at Twin Springs Farm in Ambler, Pennsylvania.

Mrs. Dailey loves her family very much. Mr. and Mrs. Dailey live in Doylestown with their daughter, Emerson; son, Ryan; and brown-and-white English bulldog, Winston. Winston does the funniest things, and you'll hear all about them at Morning Meeting and Closing Circle.

Mrs. Dailey also likes to read and spend time with her friends and family. Her favorite foods include pizza, chicken and dumplings, ice cream, and her mom's chocolate chip cookies!

In language arts this year, you will read fantastic stories and compose many of your own! You will write stories, poems, narratives, newspaper articles, advertisements, research reports, multigenre papers, and more! Mrs. Dailey will teach you some great tricks that will help improve your writing. Just wait until you see what an amazing reader and writer you can be!

In math, you will continue to explore multiplication and division. It is very important that you know these facts well! Your class will also investigate fractions, geometry, patterns, decimals, probability, measurements, and problem solving. Mrs. Dailey has some neat math projects planned for you.

During social studies, you will learn a lot about the United States and the first people who lived here. You will study U.S. history, create Pennsylvania state reports, explore the Native Americans who once lived in Bucks County, and polish your geography skills! Can you believe that by the end of 4th grade you will know all your state capitals, continents, and oceans?!

In science, you will learn about sound and light, ecosystems, rocks and minerals, and electricity. You will be able to do some amazing hands-on experiments! There are many things you'll learn in class that you can show your family; they will be amazed at what you can do!

Do you like field trips? As a 4th grader, your first field trip will be to the Churchville Nature Center, where we will spend all day walking trails and learning about nature. We may even go to Harrisburg, our state capital, in the spring.

You will have a great year in 4th grade with Mrs. Dailey. Be sure to let her know if you have any questions about anything this year. She is happy to help you!

her early days of teaching that shares both personal facts about herself and information about academics and field trips. You can read your article aloud to your class or hand out a copy to each student. This activity is an excellent way to share a bit about yourself with students, celebrate some of the fun things they can look forward to, and outline expectations for the upcoming year. If you want to gauge your students' reading comprehension and writing skills at this early point in the year, you could add a few questions at the end of the article for students to answer.

Learn About Students and Their Learning

For the rest of the first week of school, implement activities that give you insight into who students are and their learning preferences. For example, asking them to complete a creative writing assignment about themselves allows you to see how they work independently and how much work they can produce in a certain amount of time. This activity can also give you the opportunity to review expectations and praise students who successfully complete the assignment.

Next, have students complete an activity in pairs so you can see how they work with partners. For example, you can have them play a math game using dice to see how competitive they are or engage in a reading task together to see how they interact. Put them in different situations and observe where they excel and where they struggle. Insights from these activities can help you later when you are planning for partner or group work as part of your lessons.

You might also want to see how students approach classroom discussions or hands-on activities. Provide them with a variety of assignments so you can get a good idea of how they learn and work together. Remember to always reinforce your expectations and routines before and after each of these activities. This could be as simple as saying, "I love how Michael pushed in his chair before walking to another part of the classroom" or "We are getting quicker at our transitions from one activity to another. I am proud of us!" Reinforcing routines and expectations may feel repetitive, but it will pay off big time once it has made your classroom routine systems and structures second nature to your class. This will in turn increase your instructional time with students. If you know that your students already struggle with behavior issues, start with more structured activities before moving toward more open-ended activities. The key is to see how students handle the activities and then adjust them accordingly.

Always Have Something Up Your Sleeve

No matter how meticulously you plan, something is bound to catch you off guard. Perhaps students fly through a lesson way faster than you anticipated, or the photocopier did not work in the morning so you couldn't make copies of an activity. For this reason, it is vital to always have a backup plan.

As Anita Archer and Charles Hughes remind us in their book *Explicit Instruction* (2011), we must "avoid the void, for [students] will fill it!" (p. 111). Consider having a backup stash of quick games, icebreakers, or challenges ready to fill these awkward gaps. You might even keep photocopied activities on hand that you know students will find engaging. There are often a few students in class who complete assignments before everyone else, so have a plan in place for them, too.

Remember That Sometimes, Too Much Is a Good Thing

You may find that you over-plan for this first week and don't get through what you thought you would. This is completely normal—in fact, it's a good thing! You *want* to slow down and take your time setting up expectations and routines, giving constant reminders and praise, and teaching explicitly. As you learn about your students and reflect on this knowledge, you will inevitably need to make some changes to your plan, and that is OK, too! Just be flexible, be ready to pivot when necessary, and stay open to new learning. Students do not know what you have planned for tomorrow, so adapt as you go and pretend it is all part of your master plan.

LESSONS LEARNED

Every year, I pivot during my first week in school. I usually have to let go of something I had planned to do due to time constraints, and I know that it's always better to slow down and do things thoroughly rather than rush them. Monitoring and adjusting in Week 1 is perfect practice for the monitoring and adjusting you'll do throughout the upcoming school year!

—Suzanne

Don't Forget to Enjoy Yourself

Teaching should be fun. Though these first few days may feel stressful at times, that's actually a testament to how much you care. Remember, students give back to you what you give to them. Take the time to laugh with them, learn about them, and get to know them. The quickest way to their minds is through their hearts.

Be Kind Outside the Classroom

Our students are still our students beyond the classroom walls. You will connect with them in the hallways, at recess, or as they're getting on the bus, and we recommend seeing these times as opportunities to get to know your students better. Simple actions such as smiling at students and giving them fist bumps as they walk by are great ways to let them know that you see them and that you're happy they're there. This can be especially powerful for students who are having a tough day or struggling to fit in. Be that teacher who is aware of those who are struggling to find connections at school. Make a point of going out of your way to check in with them and spend time with them if they are alone. Sometimes we are the only connections they have, especially early in the year.

LESSONS LEARNED

At the beginning of the school year when I returned to teaching, I found it difficult watching the students connect with everyone except me. I could see the excitement they had seeing their former teachers and giving them fist bumps and sharing inside jokes. I expressed my concern to a fellow teacher who confessed that he had felt the same way when he'd first arrived at the school a couple of years before. He assured me that the connections would come and that I just had to keep smiling and putting myself out there. Sure enough, several months into the year, I was hearing my name in the hallways, joking with students, and dapping kids up. It just took a bit of time to build trust with students and for them to get to know me, too.

—Rob

Set Classroom Expectations

In Suzanne's new-teacher program, the amazing special education program specialists walk teachers through creating effective classroom rules and expectations. This section captures some of the magic positive behavioral interventions and supports they have taught us.

When setting classroom expectations, try to involve your students in the process. This makes them feel more invested in *meeting* these expectations, and it's a great way to show you value their ideas. (Tip: After your class has set the expectations, create a slide listing them that you can pull up whenever you present a slideshow.) Do not rush through this activity; make sure you give it the time it deserves. It is important that you establish clear expectations and post them somewhere in your room as an anchor chart (or a slide) and refer to them daily for the first couple of weeks.

Although you should be co-creating expectations with your students, you also know best which ones are most important for a successful classroom. Often, you can guide students into coming up with these ideas, but if you can't, make sure to add them yourself and emphasize their importance. For example, the expectation that one person talks at a time is nonnegotiable, whereas choosing which hand gesture students should use to signal their understanding is more flexible.

LESSONS LEARNED

When I returned to teaching, I implemented a behavior management system that I'd used for many years. My previous students loved this system, and they fully bought into it. So I set it up like I usually do, explained it to my new students, and invited them to give it a try. By the end of the first month, I could feel the buy-in was not there, but I continued with the system. After months of trying to make it work, I eventually came to the realization that I needed to move on and try something new. So I did. In a class meeting, my students and I discussed strategies that might work better, and we are trying one of those now. The moral of the story is that all groups are different, and sometimes you need to cut your losses and try something new.

—Rob

When you think about all the things you want your students to do, your list may be 55 items long. But we all understand that having too many rules in place is ineffective. Ideally, you will have three to five simple classroom rules that

- Are stated in positive terms,
- Use clear and concise language,
- Are observable and measurable, and
- Are age-appropriate.

Following are a few examples of classroom rules. As you read them, consider whether they meet the criteria outlined above:

1. Walk when moving from place to place in the classroom.
2. Treat others with respect.
3. No hitting.

The first rule listed meets all four criteria. The second rule, though stated in positive terms and clear language, may not always be observable and may not be measurable, because "respect" means different things to different people. This rule is not especially age-appropriate either, since respect looks different depending on age and environment. It also lacks specificity about the targeted behavior; for example, if you want students to mind their language, the rule might be cast as "Use school-appropriate language when speaking with others." (Even though *school-appropriate* is somewhat subjective, it's less open to interpretation than a term like *kind* or *nice*.) The third rule meets the last three criteria but is not stated in positive terms; a more effective rule would be something like "Please keep your hands, feet, and belongings to yourself."

Figure 2.3 provides some space for you to brainstorm possible classroom rules for your upcoming year and assess how well each one meets the four criteria.

Practice and Reinforce!

There's "teacher tired" and then there's "first-week-of-school teacher tired." Yes, it can be tiring to repeatedly remind students of rules and expectations, or to celebrate whenever an expectation is met. But we promise that spending time on these things up front is well worth it both for you and for

FIGURE 2.3 **Brainstorming Classroom Rules**

Possible Rule	Stated in Positive Terms?	Clear and Concise Language?	Observable and Measurable?	Age-Appropriate?

your students. Taking the time to ensure students understand the rules at the beginning of the year will buy you more instructional time the rest of the year.

Simply reading the rules with your class isn't enough to ensure they stick. Instead, we suggest following these steps:

1. **Present the rule.** "Our first rule is 'Walk when moving from place to place in the classroom.'"
2. **Explain why it's important.** "This rule is important because it helps keep our learning community safe."
3. **Model how to follow the rule with three to five examples.** Walk between desks, walk to the pencil sharpener, and walk to the door when class is over. Overtly modeling for students allows them to see and better understand classroom expectations.
4. **Provide three to five "nonexamples"—instances of the rule not being followed.** Run to the door, skip to the front board, and speed-walk to a student's desk. You can also show a video of a nonexample.

5. **Practice the rule.** Invite students to practice the rule together in real time. For example, say, "Let's practice walking from our desks to the door quietly and respectfully."
6. **Reinforce the rule.** Acknowledge when students follow the rule and correct them when they don't. It's most effective to do this in real time.

Another way to reinforce expectations is to maintain consistent classroom routines that follow the rules you've set. Consider establishing clear routines for students related to the following:

- Arriving to class
- Taking attendance
- Going to the bathroom
- Managing classroom resources (e.g., sharpening pencils, charging laptops, storing tablets)
- Speaking during whole-class discussions
- Submitting work
- Transitioning between activities or classrooms
- Asking for help
- Finishing classroom assignments early
- Borrowing or returning items
- Looking for lost items
- Doing independent work
- Maintaining a reasonable volume
- Dealing with unexpected interruptions (e.g., fire drills, the teacher being called out for a phone call)
- Wrapping things up (e.g., clearing desks and putting chairs away)

Once you have established classroom routines, reinforce them until you feel like a broken record. Although this may feel excessive at times, repetition helps turn routines into habits.

One surprising quirk about students is that they tend to do exactly what we ask them to do—but only if we are clear and explicit about what that is. For example, if you hold something up in class and ask, "Who knows what this is?" students are likely to all answer you at once unless you make your expectations explicit ("Raise your hand if you can tell me what this is"). It is a small adjustment, but one that can really affect how your lesson turns out.

When students are not meeting expectations, remember to address the behavior, not the person. For instance, instead of "You are being disruptive," you can say, "Throwing paper is not acceptable in our classroom." It takes time to get students where you want them, so expect that not all your expectations will be met every day. Remember that each day is a clean slate and try not to hold past misbehavior against students. They are just learning, and focusing on their missteps will slow down their progress.

One of the best ways to celebrate students who *are* meeting your expectations is to make a positive phone call home. Both students and parents love getting these, which builds rapport and encourages students to continue the positive behavior. (If you want to "level up" this strategy, you can ask the *student* to call home and report their great behavior!)

Be Proactive: Nothing Beats a Well-Planned Lesson

The power of a well-planned lesson is often overlooked when discussing classroom management. If our lessons are engaging and students move seamlessly between learning opportunities, the management usually takes care of itself. But if we are struggling through lessons and lack confidence, management issues are likely to crop up.

To prepare for lessons, think through how long each part of a lesson will take and pay attention to how much time students will spend listening to you versus working and learning. Make sure your technology is working and your handouts are ready, too, as time spent scrambling at the start of a lesson can also lead to management issues.

LESSONS LEARNED

I once had a colleague who was great at classroom management, and she always remained calm and spoke quietly. I found her control over her class remarkable. One day I asked her, "What is your classroom management secret?" She smiled and answered, "Planning." She always planned with her students in mind, knowing that if she planned her lessons well, they would not have time to misbehave.

—Rob

It takes time to develop great classroom management skills, and there's always more to learn. A good start is to build relationships with students, be explicit with expectations, praise students like crazy, and learn to adapt to the dynamics of the class in front of you.

Teach with Love to Build a Lasting Classroom Community

In his book *Big Potential*, Shawn Achor (2018) likens human collaboration to lightning bugs synchronizing their flashes to attract others. "Like the lightning bugs," he writes, "when we learn to coordinate and collaborate with those around us, we all begin to shine brighter—both as individuals and as part of a greater ecosystem" (pp. 17–18). As educators, one of our primary goals is to foster a strong, united classroom community that brings us together and helps us achieve our shared goals. While building this sense of community is an ongoing effort throughout the year, it begins on the very first day. Take the time on Day 1 to learn how to pronounce students' names correctly and ask questions that show you are interested in getting to know more about them. As the teacher, you play a key role in establishing the tone of the community you aim to build. Actions often speak louder than words, so approach every interaction with intentionality and consistency, demonstrating respect, kindness, and empathy. The more students see these values in action, the more likely they are to mirror them in their own behaviors.

LESSONS LEARNED

For the first day of school, I decorate the classroom as I would a New Year's Eve party, with streamers and signs that say "Happy New Year," and discuss the year's goals with students as though they are New Year's resolutions. It's a joyful way to begin the year. Then, in January, when we return from winter break and it's the *actual* new year, we reflect on the goals we set in September and revise them for the second half of the year.

—Suzanne

It's important to have a clear idea of what a great community looks like going into the school year. For most educators, a great community is based on kindness, mutual respect, trust, and effective collaboration. Although it can be tempting to present your vision of community to students on an anchor chart, it is more effective to involve students in the process so they will be more likely to invest in it. When students have a voice in creating their classroom community, when they see their ideas being recorded and used, they will feel heard and valued.

LESSONS LEARNED

On the first day of school, I ask my students, "What would make this an amazing school year?" To guide their thinking, I post anchor charts labeled Teacher, Peers, You, Classwork, and School Activities around the room. Working in small groups, students go from chart to chart adding their ideas about what would contribute to a great year. Afterward, we come together as a whole group to discuss how we might collaborate as a community to bring this shared vision to life. These anchor charts remain displayed in our classroom and serve as a reference during celebrations, class meetings, and challenging moments.

—Rob

Develop a Mission Statement

In 2007, Suzanne's 4th grade classroom worked with ChartHouse Learning to create a class mission statement through its FISH! for Schools curriculum. This curriculum was modeled after the famous Pike Place fish market in Seattle, Washington, which draws crowds from all over the world to witness its fun, energetic, friendly culture. ChartHouse created a curriculum for schools that brought the FISH! Philosophy's (FISH! Blog, 2023) four principles—Choose your attitude, Make their day, Be there, and Play—to the classroom. Co-creating a mission statement at the beginning of the year was a powerful way for the class to put this curriculum in practice.

When crafting a class mission statement with your students, you can start by asking them the following five questions:

1. Why are we here?
2. What do we want to accomplish?
3. How will we treat others?
4. How will we treat property?
5. How do we want to feel (and help others feel) at school?

Depending on the grade level, you may ask all the questions at once or tackle one or two a day. Ask students to independently reflect on and respond to each question on a separate sticky note. Once all questions have been answered, gather the sticky notes and place them into five piles (one for each question). Assign a group of students to each pile and have them summarize the sticky notes using these language frames:

1. We are here to ______________.
2. We want to accomplish ______________.
3. We will treat others ______________.
4. We will treat property ______________.
5. We want to feel and help others feel ______________.

Give students five to seven minutes to review the responses in their pile and come up with a sentence that represents the class. When they are done, it's time to combine the summary sentences together into a mission statement. Figure 2.4 features examples of a mission statement worded appropriately for three different grade levels.

A classroom mission statement helps to reinforce expected behaviors. For example, if you notice a student pushing in a classmate's chair on the way out of class, you might say, "Thank you, Jamie, for treating property as if it were your own." In some classrooms, students even recite the mission statement aloud at the beginning of every day.

Unite Your Students

Here are just a few strategies you can use to actively build a unified classroom community right from the start:

- Create a class name and logo. You can even have a logo contest!
- Pick or create a class mantra together that focuses on building a positive identity as a class.
- Music brings people together. Compile a classroom song playlist. This offers a great opportunity to discuss acceptance of others' likes

FIGURE 2.4 **Sample Classroom Mission Statements**

Kindergarten

PM MISSION STATEMENT

We are here to LEARN and have FUN. We will be KIND and CARING. We will RESPECT property. We want to feel SAFE, HAPPY, and WELCOME!!!

Sign below

Elementary

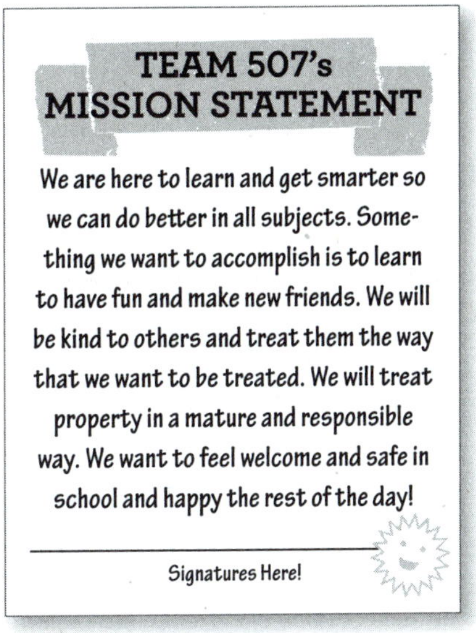

TEAM 507's MISSION STATEMENT

We are here to learn and get smarter so we can do better in all subjects. Something we want to accomplish is to learn to have fun and make new friends. We will be kind to others and treat them the way that we want to be treated. We will treat property in a mature and responsible way. We want to feel welcome and safe in school and happy the rest of the day!

Signatures Here!

Secondary

"We are here to learn, make new friends, and build character. We want to accomplish learning and have fun while we're doing it. We will treat others the way we want to be treated and with respect. We will treat property with respect and care. We want to feel and help others feel happy, confident, proud, and special."

TEAM 8-2

and interests. You can then have the playlist on in the background while students work, or use songs from the playlist to transition between or within lessons (e.g., "This song is three and a half minutes long. By the time it's done, you should have your book open to page 23 and be ready to go.").

Whatever activities you decide to use, make sure students feel that they've had a voice in developing them.

Add Community Building into Your Timetable

Community building is not something that you address in the first week and then move on from; rather, you should work on building community throughout the year. Here are some examples of strategies you can use to regularly prioritize this aspect of teaching:

- **Community circle.** Start each *week* with a community circle, where students share about their weekend or something that is going on in their lives.
- **Morning meetings.** Start each *day* with a meeting or check-in to see how students are feeling.
- **Closing circle.** *End* each day with a quick check-in to summarize the learnings of the day and encourage an optimistic viewpoint. For example, you can take three to five minutes at the end of each day to have students "scan for the good"; that way, when they go home and a parent asks, "How was your day?" they will be likely to respond with something specific and positive. This strategy helps you build your credibility as a new teacher while fostering a positive connection between school and home.
- **Class meetings.** Every *month,* schedule a lengthier class meeting where students can share their appreciations or concerns and ask questions. Planning a general agenda beforehand, setting norms, and using sentence starters are all ways to help the conversation stay in a productive place.
- **Cooperative games.** You can connect your lessons to classroom community goals by incorporating cooperative games (e.g., a math fact relay, a breakout room). This is a great way to foster teamwork, increase class morale, and have fun at the same time!

LESSONS LEARNED

One of my favorite ways to build community is through small movement breaks that I call "energizers." These are just moments throughout the day that get

students up and moving to reset their attention. I will ask students who are having a great day (academically or behaviorally) to choose an energizer from various options. Two of our favorites are "Hi, My Name Is Joe," a fun chant that adds on moves with every verse, and "Cha-Cha Slide," a spirited song and dance. (You can find energizers suitable for all ages at GoNoodle.com.)

—Suzanne

Create Opportunities to Connect

As the weeks progress, community building deepens through shared experiences and intentional practices. Collaborative group work, class discussions, and celebrations of individual and collective milestones all play a role in reinforcing a sense of belonging. It's in these moments that students learn they are not alone and that their success is intertwined with the success of those around them. Much like the synchronized flashes of lightning bugs, their collective brilliance grows brighter when they work together.

Tackle Adversity Together

When the inevitable conflicts arise in your classroom, look to them as opportunities to grow as a class and support one another. Whether you wait until the class meeting or pause your lesson to address an issue, remember to connect back to your classroom goals and expectations. Be sure to give students the opportunity to voice their opinions and come up with possible solutions. As educators, we often jump in to resolve things ourselves so we can get back to teaching. But sometimes you need to invest the time to ensure that minor issues do not become major issues.

LESSONS LEARNED

One staple in my classroom is the "Ask Mrs. Dailey" box. It's a shoebox wrapped in colorful paper on my desk. Students can slip notes with questions or concerns into the box, either anonymously or with their names. This strategy gives students a predictable place to share their thoughts privately if they don't feel comfortable doing so aloud or in front of the class. It also shows them that I am always available to listen to their thoughts.

—Suzanne

Continue to Build Community Outside the Classroom

There are many opportunities throughout the year to build community in a different setting. Encourage your students to join school clubs and attend extracurricular events. These different environments allow students to interact in new ways and with new people. If you have the time, get involved yourself. The relationships you build in these environments can be a lot different than the ones you experience in the classroom.

We also encourage you to look for ways to get out into the community together as a class. Whether it's a class trip to a historic site or volunteering at a local charity, these experiences bring students together and help them see one another in a new light.

Maximize Your Mentor

Here is a list of questions to ask your mentor at this point in the school year:

- What is our grading philosophy?
- How are grades tracked?
- What edtech tools can help with student engagement or teacher productivity?
- What are the expectations for parent conferences? Can you walk me through a typical conference?
- Can I observe you or another colleague while you teach?
- If I am sick, how do I call out? Can you show me a good example of plans for a substitute teacher? Where would I keep emergency sub plans?
- Can you provide feedback on my classroom setup? (Wait a few weeks after school starts so you have had time to make adjustments.)
- Can you proofread my emails to large groups or challenging parents?
- Can you help me talk through a challenging parent phone call?

Take Care of School-Year You

The students are here. You've worked tirelessly to establish expectations, reinforce desired behavior, build relationships, and get started with the curriculum. This is a lot! As a teacher, you have worked hard, so it's time to take care of your own needs. For some of us, it's relatively easy to bracket off school and lean into our personal lives, but for others it's more challenging. Regardless of how you are wired, here are two small shifts we invite you to consider.

Try a Weekend Wish

As Nedra Glover Tawwab, author of *Set Boundaries, Find Peace* (2021), observes, "Many of us are not practicing self-care. We are practicing after-care. After-care is what we do once we are diminished and depleted. Pre-care is preventative. It is used to stay well and maintain your peace" (Tawwab, 2022). One way to lean into pre-care at this busy time of year is simply to ask yourself, "What is my weekend wish?" before the weekend arrives. Doing this gives you a chance to envision what you will need to feel rejuvenated by the time you return to school on Monday. It could be something simple: going for a long run, grabbing coffee with a friend, or just carving out time to be alone, unplug, and create.

Start a "Yay, Me!" Folder

We tend to remember the critical feedback we receive more than the positive feedback. Thankfully, in your first few years of teaching, you are bound to receive positive feedback from colleagues, students, administrators, and parents. We encourage you to create a folder (both in your email inbox and as an actual paper folder) labeled "Yay, Me!" Whenever you receive positive emails or letters of gratitude, place them in the folder. These can then serve as overt reminders of the good work you are doing, reminding you of your purpose and legacy. You will be so proud of the words of affirmation you collect not only in your first few years, but also in years to come.

CHAPTER 2 CHECKLIST

We hope this chapter has encouraged you to think of new ways to connect with your students and begin building a great classroom community in the first couple weeks of school. Take your time to create the conditions for students to be happy and successful in your class this year.

Happiness and Success for Your Students and Classroom

- ☐ Prioritize greeting students at the door as they enter your classroom.
- ☐ Have some go-to greetings ready.
- ☐ Plan activities that allow students to get to know one another better as you learn about them.
- ☐ Think of three to five classroom expectations to share.
- ☐ Co-create a mission statement as a class that reflects classroom goals and expectations.
- ☐ Consider how to include students in community-building activities.
- ☐ Plan ways to explain classroom routines and praise students when they follow them.
- ☐ Collect data on how students learn best.
- ☐ Encourage teamwork and unity among students.
- ☐ Plan for manageable ways to check in with students and collect their thoughts.
- ☐ To set yourself up for future success, plan activities that keep students engaged.
- ☐ Ask your mentor any questions that you need answered at this time of the school year.

✓

Happiness and Success for You

- ☐ Be kind to yourself. Not everything will go as planned, and that is OK.
- ☐ Don't reinvent the wheel! Ask colleagues if they have activities you can modify for your students.
- ☐ If someone offers help, accept it!
- ☐ Lean into new professional friends who support you and make you feel good.
- ☐ Enjoy getting to know your students—have fun and smile!
- ☐ Practice pre-care and self-care by coming up with weekend wishes.
- ☐ Start a "Yay, Me!" folder.

✓

CHAPTER

The School Year Is Underway!

Sustaining Classroom Happiness and Success

In a perfect world, our classrooms would have minimal disruptions. Students would be engaged, display desired behaviors, and have enough time to accomplish each task. Although we know we won't get that *all* the time, this chapter discusses ways to get there *most* of the time by proactively setting a positive tone for the upcoming day or class period.

Implement Positivity Pauses

There will be times in your school day when students need a little reset. These are natural opportunities to teach students to train their minds to bend toward a more optimistic viewpoint. One strategy we have used for this purpose is implementing "positivity pauses" throughout the day. A positivity pause is simply a two- to three-minute pause during which students think about their past, present, or future and scan for the good or for what's going well.

Following are some of our favorite prompts for engaging students in positivity pauses. You may also choose to use these as discussion starters for partners or groups or ask students to write responses in their journals.

- What's an ordinary moment that brings you great joy?
- Think about a time you just felt lucky.
- What's something in your life that turned out better than you imagined?
- What are you grateful for today?
- What is something you are looking forward to?
- What intentional act of kindness do you want to perform this week?
- Name a positive emotion you experienced [yesterday/last week/last month].
- Think of a time when someone was thankful for something you did or said.
- What is an accomplishment you are proud of?
- What is something you didn't know much about a year ago that you now *love*?
- What's something you recently learned about yourself?

You can also use sentence starters:

- I am grateful for ________________
- I am thankful for ________________.
- Today was a good day because ________________.
- It was fun when ________________.
- I appreciate ________________.
- I am happy because ________________.
- I am lucky because ________________.
- I'm thankful I learned ________________.

During positivity pauses, happiness chemicals like dopamine and serotonin are released in the body as students reflect on positive things. These chemicals put students in a calm and relaxed state that makes them more open to learning.

Distribute an Interest Inventory

Now that the school year is underway, you are hopefully starting to get a good grasp on the students in your class. There are usually some students who are desperate for connection, and you will quickly get to know them—they won't be hard to find. But for many other students, making connections will take time, effort, and creativity. If you haven't done so yet, take some time to have students complete an interest inventory so you can learn information about them that might lead to new connections. Here are some examples of good interest survey questions:

- What is your favorite [band/TV show/type of candy/etc.]?
- What gets you pumped up and motivated?
- What is the single most important thing to you?
- If you could have dinner with anyone, who would it be?
- What do you do for fun?
- What is your dream vacation?
- What scares you or stresses you out?

Take the time to read students' responses to the survey carefully and revisit them throughout the year if you are struggling to connect. If possible, embed some of their interests into your lessons or class discussions. By doing so, you will not only better engage students in the lesson but also plant the seed for more conversations down the line.

LESSONS LEARNED

At a grade 8 graduation, I had a student come up to me and say, "You know what meant the most to me this year? The fact that you pretended to be interested in horses all year just to get to know me. It really showed me you cared about me." I had learned about this student's love of horses from an interest survey I'd conducted on the first day of school. I guess I wasn't as slick as I thought, but bringing up her interests made her happy to be in my class and willing to get to know me better.

—Rob

Lean Into Intentional Interactions

You will build most of your connections with students outside the lessons you are teaching: in the hallways, on recess duty, during extracurriculars, and so on. These are times when you can joke with students, have random conversations with them, and show them that you are invested in them beyond the classroom. Look for opportunities in these nonteaching times to connect with students you don't often get an opportunity to connect with. Ask them questions and take time to listen. Look for common interests or share stories that will help them relate to you.

Do not give up on a student if you find it difficult to form a connection with them. Take it as a challenge and be persistent—some students take a long time and many interactions to open up. Eventually, they will start to look forward to these interactions, and that is when the true connections will start to form.

LESSONS LEARNED

This year, I had to work really hard to connect with a particular student. It took almost four months before I landed on the breakthrough: butter chicken. I was eating it in the library when he walked in to ask me a question. He looked at my fork and said that what I was eating looked good. Jokingly, I extended my fork to him, and to my surprise, he picked the chicken off the fork and ate it. The next time I had butter chicken, I made him a little dish of it. Before I knew it, we had a special handshake that we practice all the time. I am so glad I never gave up on making this connection with him, as it became a highlight of my year.

—Rob

Let Them Get to Know You

Whether in informal hallway conversations or in the middle of a lesson or class meeting, share your stories and personal experiences with students. Opening up to them makes them more likely to open up to you. Many students think of teachers as robots that live in their classrooms' closets, emerging only to teach during the day; sharing about our lives helps to humanize us in their eyes.

At the same time, we need to be careful not to overshare with students. Remember, in this professional setting, they are our students, not our friends. This can be especially difficult when teaching older students, but it's important to be firm about maintaining this boundary.

There will be times when students don't ask you directly about your personal life but instead seek out the information online. Be sure to diligently monitor your social media accounts and scrub anything that might be considered objectionable or controversial. Both of us know of colleagues who have been questioned about their online posts, so this is also a proactive way to protect your professional reputation.

LESSONS LEARNED

I am very particular about the photos and artifacts I have in my classroom to let students know a little more about me. There are photos of my family and favorite places I've traveled to, as well as pictures of books I love to read and other things that make me happy. I also strategically leave a few notes and thank-you cards from previous students around to show that positive relationships with my students are important to me; it sets a nice tone in a low-stakes way.

—Suzanne

Over time, students will begin to let their guard down and see the real you. Hopefully, you will be someone they look for in the hallways and feel comfortable confiding in when they are struggling. Make sure they know that you are available for them. If you know they are having a tough time with something, offer your support and make time for them. It's also very important to follow through on any promises you make and advocate for students whenever you can. It takes a lot of effort to build trust, and very little to break it. Students are looking for someone who is understanding, patient, and reliable, so show them that you are the caring adult they want and need in their lives.

LESSONS LEARNED

At the beginning of the year, one of my students got into a fight before school and was sent to the office. As soon as I found out, I went to the office to see him. I could tell he thought I was going to be mad at him, but instead I said, "Being in a fight is scary. Are you all right?" We talked about it, and from that day on, he showed me a great deal of respect and made some very positive changes to his behavior. I even selected him for our recognition assembly for the way he dealt with the situation by owning his behavior and making better decisions. In the end, a negative event helped to strengthen our connection.

—Rob

Conduct a Classroom Audit

As the year progresses, it's always a good idea to periodically evaluate how things are going. Use a classroom audit to check in with your students now and then to elicit their thoughts on what is working for them in the classroom. We've found it effective to encourage students to assess their learning around the time they get their report cards. Asking questions like the following can provide you with meaningful feedback:

- What time of day do you feel most productive?
- What time of day do you feel most calm and balanced?
- Where do you like to get your work done most of the time?
- Do you prefer to sit near others or on your own?
- Does the lighting in our room help you focus?
- If you could change one thing about our classroom layout, what would it be?
- What do you like best about our classroom furniture, decorations, or organization system?
- Draw your ideal classroom, using mainly the furniture we already have.

Consider the Magic Ratio

In her book *High Conflict,* Amanda Ripley (2021) shares the results of a study from the Gottman Institute (Gottman & Levenson, 1992) that can help us proactively connect with others. This study found that stable, happy relationships tend to have a "magic ratio" of five positive interactions for every negative interaction. This 5:1 ratio helps sustain healthy and productive connections in both professional and personal contexts. As you get to know your students over the next few weeks, and especially as you reinforce classroom expectations, keep the magic ratio in mind.

Pay Attention to Bids for Connection

The Gottman Institute has a wildly high success rate helping individuals repair or strengthen their relationships with one another. One of its recommendations is for us to notice when someone is giving us a "bid for connection"—that is, "any attempt from one to another for attention, affirmation, affection, or any other positive connection" (Brittle, 2024, para. 5). As with bidding in an auction, a bid for connection is essentially an offer—in this case, to connect. Bids can come in any number of forms, from a simple smile to a request for advice.

Some things we see as annoying interruptions may actually be bids for connection: a student asking us to watch a TikTok video during the transition between classes, for example, or asking, "Like my new shoes?" while we scramble to submit attendance. Trying to notice when a student is making a bid for connection can help us be a bit more intentional with our limited time and energy.

Remember These Seven Words to Brighten a Student's Day

There's a great Toni Morrison quote from her 2000 appearance on *The Oprah Winfrey Show* (OWN, 2011): "Does your face light up when your child enters the room?" We would like to think our faces light up when we see anyone we care about, but we don't think they would light up each and every time. One way we can help brighten the faces (and spirits) of the students around us is by saying seven simple words:

I saw this and thought of you.

When we say this to a student, their immediate thought is, "Ooh, I wonder why they thought of me!" and they are instantly invested. This seven-word phrase is an instant connection builder—not only with our students, but with practically anyone else, too. Look for the softened face; listen for the tiny sigh; watch for the tiny, upturned smile and brightened eyes.

Bring some light to their day, seven words at a time.

Reinforce Expectations

In the first weeks of school, you worked hard to establish expectations and build relationships with your students. Regardless of how well this has gone so far, the work is not done. Creating and maintaining a positive classroom environment is not something you focus on just in the first few weeks of school; it is a continuous process that you will work on all year.

As Simon Sinek (2018) notes, "[Success] is not about the events; it is not about intensity; it's about consistency." Even if we do a great job outlining our expectations and routines in Week 1, it does not mean that we will always achieve our desired results. Managing a classroom is like moving a large boulder: It can be hard to get started, but once you get it moving in the right direction, it gets a lot easier.

A study by Rumfola (2017) revealed that students who received positive reinforcement from teachers were 68 percent more likely to follow classroom expectations than those who didn't. Sometimes positive reinforcement is as easy as using positive language (e.g., "Great job, Lauren, thanks for coming in and going right to your desk. You as well, Reid."). Rather than pointing out when students are *not* meeting expectations, focus on celebrating when they *are*. One good way to make positive reinforcement a habit is to start each day reflecting on what students did well the day before. By highlighting positive behavior and celebrating successes, you set a positive tone for the rest of the day.

LESSONS LEARNED

I was working with a new teacher who was struggling with classroom management. We decided to co-create new expectations with her class. Her students did a great job identifying five areas they needed to focus on. To help the class consistently reflect on their progress, we made a slide featuring a checklist of the five expectations, which the teacher would project during class. Throughout the day, she would check off the boxes on the slide as students met expectations. The students were so excited about this strategy, they would run up to me and excitedly announce, "We got four out of five, Mr. D!"

—Rob

Remember: Just Because You Post It Doesn't Mean They'll Follow It

Anything you post on the walls of your classroom eventually just becomes window dressing unless you use it properly. Once you've posted your classroom expectations, make a point of drawing students' attention to them when you are addressing their behavior. Remember to do this when they are meeting expectations as well as when they are not (e.g., "Class, we nailed these expectations today. Everyone was where they were supposed to be and doing what they were supposed to be doing. Awesome job!").

Implement a Reward System

To keep students engaged in meeting classroom expectations, consider implementing a reward system. This is a fun and positive way to motivate students. Rewards can take various forms, such as points (as in a game), privileges (e.g., extra break time), or recognition (e.g., certificates, shout-outs, leadership opportunities). Of course, the end goal is for students to become intrinsically motivated, but a reward system can help you get the ball rolling in that direction.

Promote Peer Recognition and Gratitude

Another effective way to reinforce positive behavior is through peer recognition. Providing students with the opportunity to recognize one another for their contributions to the class builds community and reinforces desired behaviors. Here are some ideas to get you started:

- Provide students with cards they can fill out highlighting a classmate's positive behavior in the classroom. Share the cards with the whole class.
- Supply "gratitude cards" that students can fill out and post on the walls of the classroom. Take time to highlight new gratitude cards whenever they are posted.
- Start your class meetings by opening up the floor to students who would like to express appreciation to classmates or to the teacher.

LESSONS LEARNED

One of the turning points for me this year was starting classroom meetings. I did not start until around the fourth month of school, as I did not predict my class participating well in them. To my surprise, these meetings became pivotal to our success as a class. At first, my students were too shy to recognize and appreciate other students. Now, just several months later, they are doing a great job recognizing others. Even students who I never thought would share an appreciation are doing so. It is bringing our class closer together and at the same time promoting the expectations we are working toward as a class.

—Rob

Build Student Leadership

Once you feel confident with your classroom management, you can start to think about classroom leadership and envision how to celebrate the many skills and talents in your class. At this point, you should have a pretty good idea of who the natural leaders are in your classroom. They are most likely the ones who are good at expressing themselves and who other students listen to and follow. These natural leaders play an important role in the classroom, but there are many more leaders sitting in those seats who need your encouragement to shine. Part of building a positive classroom community is finding ways to bring out the best in each student. By nurturing all students and inviting them to use their unique skills and talents, you can build their confidence, increase their engagement, and positively influence the decisions of others in the classroom. Here are some strategies for promoting student leadership in your class:

- Assign your students specific responsibilities in group projects (e.g., project manager, researcher, presenter) to encourage leadership in different capacities.
- Assign classroom roles (e.g., class ambassador, peer mentor, materials manager) to give students a sense of ownership and responsibility.
- Teach younger students leadership skills such as patience, communication, and responsibility.
- Engage students in project-based learning. Complex school projects require students to take ownership of their learning through decision making, collaboration, and problem solving—all key leadership skills.

LESSONS LEARNED

I had a student once ask if we could try a new format for morning meeting. He had come up with different greetings and wanted to mix things up a bit. Since I try to say yes whenever I can, I told him we could try out his new ideas the next week. It turned out the other students *loved* what he had come up with. Soon I had other students asking to come up with ideas, and not only for morning meeting. Saying yes doesn't just help students feel seen and valued; it also makes them take the times when we have to say no more seriously.

—Suzanne

Teach Leadership Directly

Leadership is not just about taking charge; it is about communication, decision making, responsibility, and recognizing the contributions of others. Consider implementing direct instruction in these key leadership skills:

- **Communication.** Teach students how to articulate ideas clearly, listen actively, and give constructive feedback.

- **Decision making.** Provide opportunities for students to analyze situations, weigh options, and make informed choices.
- **Responsibility.** Assign tasks that require accountability and provide students with constructive feedback.
- **Recognizing and celebrating leadership.** Highlight both quiet and visible leaders in your class meetings as well as whenever you see them demonstrate leadership.

LESSONS LEARNED

This year I have two students in my classroom who are amazing but quiet leaders. When I acknowledged them as leaders, they were surprised, as they didn't see themselves fitting the definition of leadership. I explained to the class that these students led by example. For instance, one of them would walk into the classroom in the morning and take the chairs off the desks without being asked. Before I knew it, his classmates started doing the same thing. The other student rarely participated in classroom discussions, but whenever he did, his remarks were profound and moved the discussion forward. It is important for students like these to see that their contributions are significant. They truly are helping to build a strong class community.

—Rob

Expand Leadership Opportunities Outside the Classroom

Some students will jump at the opportunity to get involved in school activities outside the classroom, while others will be hesitant. As educators, we can play a pivotal role in giving reluctant students the confidence they need to become more involved. It can mean a lot to students for teachers to tell them they would love to see them involved in something outside class, and joining schoolwide teams, clubs, or organizations provides students with natural leadership experiences that build confidence and teamwork. If your school has a student government, you can encourage students to run for a class office or join the student council. You can also urge them to serve as "student helpers" around the school as a way of fostering their leadership skills. For example, Rob currently runs a Tech Team made up of students who help manage and troubleshoot student laptops. He has also appointed a photographer and videographer to capture some of the great things happening throughout the school.

LESSONS LEARNED

Early in my career, I worked at a school with a mentorship program in place for students who needed support. Teachers volunteered to mentor a student whom they did not teach in the classroom. We were able to select the student ourselves, so I asked to work with a grade 5 student who was being picked on by students as well as a staff member. This student did not have any friends, had very little confidence, and carried a lot of anger. During our time together, we started playing Connect Four. He was talented at the game, so I decided to create a Connect Four club as an extracurricular. Here, he formed some friendships, built up his confidence, and eventually became the school's Connect Four champ! The best part of the story? A few years later, in grade 8, he was selected as valedictorian by his peers. His speech was amazing and brought a tear to almost everyone at graduation.

—Rob

The more students you can empower to become leaders in your classroom, the easier and more fulfilling teaching becomes. As your students begin to see themselves as leaders, they will look for opportunities to help out in class, support their peers, and positively contribute to the overall culture of the classroom.

Capture and Sustain Students' Attention

Sometimes we have to get crafty to capture our students' attention, so here are some ideas for doing just that. Please know that whatever strategy you choose, you have to wait until students are focused and ready before moving on. Even if you have to wait a little bit longer than you want, wait! The time spent up front will pay off later.

Strategies for Younger Students

For younger students, consider implementing a call-and-response routine or other verbal signal for capturing attention. For example:

- Teacher: "Macaroni and cheese!" Students: "Everybody freeze!"
- Teacher: "1, 2, 3, eyes on me!" Students: "1, 2, eyes on you!"
- Teacher: "All set?" Students: "You bet!"
- "If you can hear me, put your hands on your [head/finger/nose/etc.]."
- "Active listening in 3, 2, 1!"
- Teacher: "Here comes a direction. How many times will I give this?" Students: "Once!"
- "If you can hear me, clap once. If you can hear me, clap twice. If you can hear me, clap three times [and so on until the class is quiet]." (As students become familiar with this verbal cue to quiet their voices, their challenge is to *decrease* the number of claps needed to quiet down.)

You can also use a silent physical signal. For example, you might silently move your arms around and have students mirror what you're doing; once all students are mirroring you, you know they're all listening, and you can proceed with the lesson.

Strategies for Older Students

For students in upper-elementary or secondary school, consider strategies like these:

- Clap twice and raise your hand. Wait for students to show active listening.
- Write a thought-provoking question or inspirational quote on the board and set a timer. As students enter the classroom and organize their materials, they can independently consider the question or quote. When the timer goes off, a class discussion begins, signaling the start of class.
- Designate a spot in the classroom such that if you stand there, students know they are expected to actively listen.

Note that students of any age may have IEPs that require directions to be repeated multiple times. If so, be sure to adhere to these legal guidelines when addressing those students.

Set Expectations Around Student Attention

One way to help students attend to your lessons is to make sure they clearly know what's expected of them. For example, say you are asking students to complete specific math problems on page 17 of a workbook. Instead of saying, "Please complete questions 1, 2, and 5 on page 17," you may want to say, "Everybody put a circle around question number 1, then hold your pencil in the air. Now circle question number 2," and so forth. This proactive teaching move can help students set themselves up to work independently by minimizing questions about expectations. If most students can work through these clear expectations, you will have more time to check on and support students who need some help to complete the assignment. You could even add something like "If you finish early and want a challenge, you can complete numbers 1 and 2 on page 18."

Here's another example: Say you are asking students to read an article and jot down notes. You will likely have some students jotting hardly anything down while others write extensively. To help focus students' attention on the assignment, it's important to provide clear expectations. You might try something like this:

> Teacher: "As you read the article, you will jot down at least three things you notice in the margin. Can you write more than three?"
>
> Students: "Yes!"
>
> Teacher: "Can you write fewer than three?"
>
> Students: "No!"

Circulate Around the Room

When students are far away from you, they are more likely to become distracted. For this reason, it's important not to be tied to the board or the front of the room. Move around so that you can be close to all students at some point during the lesson. This allows you to check on everyone and gives students the opportunity to seek your help when they need it. A popular way to make circulating more manageable is to invest in a wireless remote, which enables teachers to advance lesson slides from anywhere in the classroom.

To prevent students from zoning out too much, you might also consider designating different areas of the room for different parts of lessons.

For example, you can have students gather on the carpet when you model lessons, then return to their desks for independent practice. Or you might teach reading using the board in the front of the room, but teach the next topic at the side or in the back of the room.

Set Expectations for When Students Are Stuck

Wouldn't it be lovely if we gave directions and every student just magically "got it" from the jump? Unfortunately, that won't happen, but we can help students a lot by letting them know what they should do if they are stuck or confused. Let all students know beforehand what the expectation is (e.g., skip the question and come back to it later, look it up in a textbook, write the question on the board). This strategy encourages students to engage in healthy, productive struggle, working through some of their discomfort on their own before expecting the teacher to come to their rescue.

Set Expectations for When Students Are Through

Every classroom has fast finishers and slower finishers. To keep those fast finishers attending to work, it's always good practice to proactively instruct them on what to do if they finish early. Some teachers post a chart of appropriate, meaningful things for students to do in these situations.

Try to Reach Reluctant Learners

One of the most effective ways to reach students who seem hesitant to learn is to know what motivates them. Robyn Jackson (2016) refers to our strong personal motivating forces as "will drivers." In *Never Underestimate Your Teachers* (2013), she says, "[W]e are all driven by the desire for four basic feelings: autonomy, mastery, purpose, and belonging. Each of us, however, has a *primary will driver*—one of the four that matters more to us than the others and is key to our motivation" (p. 75). Once we know our students' primary will drivers, we can better meet them where they are and support their learning.

Before digging into what motivates your students, it's important to understand what motivates *you*. To do that, try the following exercise. Answer the following three questions, keeping track of which letter response you choose most often.

1. Which of the following best describes you?
   A. I do best when I have a little bit of choice in how to accomplish a task.
   B. I do best when I know I can succeed at a task.
   C. I work best when I know what I am doing matters.
   D. I work best when I can collaborate with others.
2. If you were asked to be part of a new district initiative, which of the following would be most important to you?
   A. Having guidelines in place, but also some freedom to make my own decisions
   B. Fully understanding the expectations of the initiative and being able to accomplish my work successfully
   C. Understanding why the district is leaning into this initiative
   D. Being able to collaborate with colleagues who are equally invested in the work and can help me grow professionally
3. Which of the following sentences best describes you?
   A. I can succeed at something when I have some control over what matters to me.
   B. I feel best about myself and my accomplishments when I know I have gotten really good at what I'm doing and have succeeded at my work.
   C. I do best when I am involved in work that matters to me and that I think is meaningful—both now and in the future.
   D. I work best when I am able to work alongside those who matter most to me.

As you look at your responses, do you notice a pattern? (Many of us will, but it's OK if you don't—this isn't a formal, research-backed survey!) Even if your letters don't match up perfectly, most of us feel more strongly about some of the choices than others. Let's walk through what will driver each of the letters stands for to see if the one you selected most often matches your primary or secondary will driver.

- **If you got mostly *A*s:** Your primary will driver is *autonomy*. You want to have some control over and choice in how you accomplish tasks.

Your main questions when facing a new work challenge might be "What are my choices?" and "What do I have to do?"

- **If you got mostly *B*s:** Your primary will driver is *mastery*. Essentially, you want to be successful at the task at hand. Your main questions might be "How do I do this the right way?" and "How can I be successful?"
- **If you got mostly *C*s:** Your primary will driver is *purpose*. This tends to be the most common will driver among teachers. You want to know that you are spending time and energy on things that matter and have the potential to make a difference in the long term. Your main question might be "Why am I doing this?"
- **If you got mostly *D*s:** Your primary will driver is *belonging*. It's important to you that people you care about (and who in turn value you) are involved in this work and that your presence matters. Your main questions might be "Who am I to you?" and "Who can support me in this?"

So how does knowing your primary will driver affect your work as a teacher? Let's look at a specific example. Say you're about to teach long division to your students. If your primary will driver is *purpose*, you might introduce the lesson with something like "Here is why it's important to know how to divide big numbers," and then share real-life examples of professions where long division might be used. This will show students how learning this information now will serve them in the future. If you are explaining this to a student whose primary will driver is *mastery*, they are most likely sitting there thinking, "Just tell me how to do this the right way! Show me the steps, teach me how to organize it all, and show me how to answer everything correctly." By better understanding our students' will drivers, we can more effectively meet them where they are so they can get the most out of lessons.

To know how our students are motivated, Robyn Jackson (2016) says we need to listen for two things: what questions students are asking, and what issues they're complaining about. Returning to the long division example, here's how students with different primary will drivers might react to the teacher's introduction:

- **Autonomy:** "Can I use paper and pencil instead of my laptop? It's easier for me to keep track of my numbers that way."
- **Mastery:** "Division? I just got good at multiplication!"
- **Purpose:** "Why do we need to learn this? I'd never use this in real life!"
- **Belonging:** "Who can help me practice?"

Once you get used to categorizing student reactions according to the will drivers they are likely to reflect, you almost can't *not* hear and understand where your students are coming from. This kind of understanding helps us launch units, teach lessons, and support students more efficiently and effectively.

Partner with Parents

Parents want to know what is happening in your classroom so they can talk to their child about it. Giving them a glimpse increases their trust in and rapport with you while reinforcing the idea that you are all on the same team.

Ensure Sustainable Communication

You will want to think about your preferred method of communicating with parents, but especially about what is most sustainable. We recommend teachers under-promise and over-deliver. After all, you don't want to promise to send out a weekly update every Thursday only to find that you don't have the time to do so. If the updates suddenly stop, parents will notice.

Here are a few strategies for sustaining consistent communication over the long term:

- Provide a weekly update in a take-home folder summarizing what the class accomplished that week.
- Give parents three questions to ask their child based on the week's learning. You can send them the questions directly or have students write them in an assignment book. Here is an example of three such questions from a 5th grade class:
  - — Ask me to show you how to multiply 36 by 83.
  - — Ask me to share three important events of the Boston Tea Party.
  - — Ask me to tell you about the spirit assembly and how we are showing [insert character trait] this month.

- Provide consistent updates via your district's messaging system.
- Frequently share work samples via a platform like Seesaw.

Set Email Boundaries

Email is one of the easiest ways to establish and maintain strong home-school relationships. Although you want to be able to connect with parents frequently and consistently via email, however, it's important to set some boundaries at the beginning of the school year. Remind parents that most of your time during the school day is dedicated to teaching your students, so if they email during work hours, you may not be able to respond until after school. You can also ask them for a 24-hour courtesy period for all email replies.

LESSONS LEARNED

When I taught 4th grade, one of my favorite things to do was have students call home with good news. For example, if a student did really well on an assessment after weeks of not doing so great, I'd say, "Elizabeth! This is awesome! Go call your mom!" and off she would go to call her mom and say, "Mom! I got a *B* on my math test!" Or if I noticed a student was extending help to a classmate who really needed it, I might quietly say to him, "Zach, I noticed you helping Trevor when he was stuck while reading. You were so patient and kind. Do you want to call your parents at lunch and let them know how great a friend you are?"

This is a total win any way you look at it. Parents get to be proud of their child, and students get to be proud of themselves. Parents will thank you for having students share the news in this unexpected way, and the parent-school-student relationship is strengthened.

—Suzanne

Prepare for Formal Parent-Teacher Conferences

Most districts set times aside for parents to sit down with their child's teacher and discuss students' progress, strengths, and goal areas. It's imperative to plan for these conversations, as you have limited time to capture a student's experience in school and describe their behavior and academic performance within the confines of a conference. Parents basically want to know three things:

- Do you know my kid?
- Do you like my kid?
- Are you able to convey my kid's strengths and goal areas?

Be ready to answer "yes" to these questions.

Here are a few tips for hosting a successful parent-teacher conference:

- If the conference is in person, have a welcome sign on your door so parents know they've arrived at the correct classroom. Some teachers also post something like "Please knock at your conference time" to ensure they stay on schedule.
- Have a few resources or articles available to give parents. These might focus on things like healthy study habits, homework tips, or skill practice.
- Once you decide on the "flow" of your conference, be sure all materials are ready and organized. Most teachers have a stack for each student easily accessible to them.
- Prior to the conference, some teachers like students to conduct a self-reflection about their work that semester/term/marking period. This is an opportunity for students to report on their own strengths and goal areas. These reflections can serve as a nice supplement to the conference, practically making the student another participant in it.
- If you will be discussing or providing parents with a report card, be sure to have it nearby (whether on paper or projected on a screen).
- Start the conference with something positive! For example, "I really enjoy having Ryan in class this year. He is such a great kid!" This kind of positive remark helps set parents at ease and creates the conditions for a polite conversation.
- If you want to ease into the conversation before sharing a report card or work sample, try an open-ended question like this: "Before we get into Lauren's strengths and goals, in your opinion, how is the school year going so far?"

- Discuss any behavioral issues before academic ones. Often, students' challenges with organization, active listening, and executive functioning skills affect their academic progress and success. Mentioning these challenges before discussing academic performance can provide helpful connections and insights.
- When discussing student strengths and goal areas, have recent work samples such as tests or notebooks nearby so parents can understand your conclusions.

Some districts encourage students to be present for conferences; you'll want to check with your mentor or colleagues to know if this is expected at your school. If it is and you want some time with just the parents, you can say something at the conference like, "Thanks for being here, Reid. I am going to finish up the conference by talking with Mom and Dad now, and they'll meet you in the hall when we're done. See you tomorrow in class!"

Conferences move quickly, so consider setting a timer on your phone to make sure you don't go over. If the conference is scheduled for 20 minutes, set the timer for 15 minutes to give both yourself and the parents a 5-minute warning that you're about to wrap things up.

Feel free to use the following sample conference agenda as a template for your own:

1. Welcome parents and discuss how the year is going. (2–3 min.)
2. Discuss strengths and goal areas related to behavior. (5–7 min.)
3. Discuss strengths and goal areas related to academics; where possible, link these to behavioral skills like organization, perseverance, and so on. (10 min.)
4. Thank parents and end the conference. (1 min.)

If you have less time for conferences at your school, simply reduce the time allotted to each step to fit your time frame.

Prepare for Completing Report Cards

Completing report cards can be a daunting, time-consuming task. Before you work on your first report cards, ask a colleague or mentor to show you samples for students in the following categories:

1. Performing below grade level
2. Performing at grade level
3. Performing above grade level
4. Struggling to meet behavioral expectations

(Note: If a student is struggling academically, a report card should not be the first time parents are informed of this. If it is, they are likely to be upset and reach out to you.) Once you've reviewed the samples, ask someone to sit down with you to show you exactly how to complete a report card. Most districts use a particular software program, and you'll want someone to show you how to use it efficiently.

Have Students Complete a Teacher Report Card

The best way to grow as a teacher is to be a reflective practitioner by pausing to consider your craft, identify your strengths and goal areas, and make adjustments moving forward. Report card time is a natural opportunity for students to share their feedback about your teaching. Simply put, when students get a report card, so does the teacher. Suzanne did this every year with her 4th grade students, and many of her colleagues have made it standard practice. We've found that students *love* being invited to share their opinions about their teacher and the school year, and this is an excellent way to gain insight into students' heads and hearts. Colleagues who have had students complete teacher report cards observe that this vulnerability helps strengthen teacher-student relationships and increase trust. See Figure 3.1 for an example of the teacher report card Suzanne used with her students.

Ask Parents for Feedback

You can also ask parents for their feedback on your teaching. This can be quite frightening, but it can yield insights you'd otherwise never have. Asking parents just a few questions makes them feel that we hear and value their voices and could lead to a deeper conversation about students that helps them do better in school. Consider asking parents questions like these:

- How is the school year going for your child?
- What is something positive your child has shared with you about school?

FIGURE 3.1 **Suzanne's Teacher Report Card for Students**

1. My favorite part of our school day is ________________________ because ________________________.
2. My least favorite part of our school day is ________________________ because ________________________.
3. Here are three things that I know are important to Mrs. Dailey:
   a.
   b.
   c.
4. I know Mrs. Dailey is happy when she ________________________.
5. I know Mrs. Dailey is upset when she ________________________.
6. If Mrs. Dailey were an animal, she would be a/an ________________________ because ________________________.
7. Mrs. Dailey is fair when she ________________________.
8. Mrs. Dailey could be fairer by ________________________.
9. I learn best when ________________________.
10. I could learn better if ________________________.
11. I feel important when Mrs. Dailey ________________________.
12. My favorite day of 4th grade was when ________________________.
13. My favorite book I/we read this year was ________________________ because ________________________.
14. If I could "sum up" 4th grade in one to three sentences, I would say: ________________________.

Please circle Yes, Sometimes, or No for each statement.			
Mrs. Dailey encourages me.	Yes	Sometimes	No
Mrs. Dailey motivates me to learn.	Yes	Sometimes	No
Mrs. Dailey knows a lot about me.	Yes	Sometimes	No
Mrs. Dailey yells at me.	Yes	Sometimes	No
Mrs. Dailey makes me feel good about myself.	Yes	Sometimes	No
I learn a lot from Mrs. Dailey.	Yes	Sometimes	No
Mrs. Dailey makes me laugh/smile.	Yes	Sometimes	No
Mrs. Dailey makes learning fun.	Yes	Sometimes	No
I am happy in 4th grade.	Yes	Sometimes	No
I am confident in 4th grade.	Yes	Sometimes	No
Comments/message for Mrs. Dailey (optional):			

- What is something I should consider that would help your child academically?
- What is something I should consider that would help your child socially and emotionally?
- What interests does your child have that I could try to connect to in my lessons?
- How does your child learn best?

You can also create a teacher report card for parents to complete (see Figure 3.2 for an example).

Strengthen Connections with Colleagues

When you sit in a staff meeting and look around at your new colleagues, know that they have all been where you are now. They have gone through similar struggles and had similar questions. These educators know what it is like in the first years of teaching, and (for the most part) they would love to help you succeed.

By this point in the year, you have probably met most of your colleagues. If not, take the time to introduce yourself. Make the effort to get to know each staff member; after all, you never know who will become one of "your people" in the school. Spend time in the lunchroom and other communal spaces. It is always good to take a break, share a laugh with colleagues, and form important bonds. So set a goal of showing your face several times a week and connect with fellow teachers on breaks.

One of the best ways to really get to know staff is to join in on staff activities like staff lunches, potlucks, or after-school gatherings. Educators usually attend these events to connect and have fun. You'll get to see the lighter side of colleagues and connect with them in a different way than you would while working.

Ask Your Colleagues Questions

Instead of trying to figure everything out on your own, ask questions and seek support. By asking colleagues questions, you show that you respect their advice and are open to learning from them. Here are some examples of conversation starters you can use:

FIGURE 3.2 **Suzanne's Teacher Report Card for Parents**

Dear Parents,

Teachers in the [name of district] are encouraged to create and administer parent surveys to gain a better understanding of how you feel about your child's progress and achievement. Please take a moment to complete the following survey. Thanks so much!

	Strongly Agree			**Strongly Disagree**
Professional Characteristics				
Mrs. Dailey's level of expectations is appropriate.	4	3	2	1
Mrs. Dailey demonstrates knowledge of what is taught to my child.	4	3	2	1
Mrs. Dailey makes accommodations for my child to help them learn best.	4	3	2	1
Classroom Atmosphere & Curriculum				
Mrs. Dailey gives personal help to my child if they are experiencing difficulty.	4	3	2	1
Mrs. Dailey handles problems in a positive way.	4	3	2	1
My child feels actively involved in their learning.	4	3	2	1
My child is happy at school.	4	3	2	1
Mrs. Dailey motivates my child to learn.	4	3	2	1
Mrs. Dailey encourages creative and original thinking.	4	3	2	1
Mrs. Dailey provides a variety of learning experiences in her class.	4	3	2	1
Mrs. Dailey relates to my child as an individual.	4	3	2	1
Mrs. Dailey helps my child become more independent.	4	3	2	1
Communication				
I feel comfortable communicating with Mrs. Dailey.	4	3	2	1
I feel welcome in the classroom.	4	3	2	1
I know what is happening in the classroom because of Mrs. Dailey's proactive and timely communication.	4	3	2	1
Mrs. Dailey's communications tell me what is happening in the classroom.	4	3	2	1
Assignments are graded and returned in a timely fashion.	4	3	2	1
Behavior				
Mrs. Dailey reinforces positive behavior.	4	3	2	1
I am happy with how Mrs. Dailey addresses behavior problems in the classroom.	4	3	2	1
Behavior expectations are clearly stated and understood by my child and me.	4	3	2	1
Mrs. Dailey encourages my child to take ownership of their behavior choices.	4	3	2	1
Additional comments (optional):				
Name (optional):				

- "Hey, I noticed your amazing bulletin board. Where did that idea come from?"
- "From what I hear, you're the math expert around here. Could you help me clarify something I'm struggling with?"
- "I am really interested in coaching a school team. Any chance I can come out to watch a couple practices and learn from you?"
- "I am not great with technology, but I can tell that you are. Would you have some time to show me some tricks to more effectively use tech in school?"

LESSONS LEARNED

Years ago, I was teaching in a double portable classroom when suddenly I heard someone yell "Whooo!" at the top of their lungs in the room beside me. Curious, I went to see what was happening—and I could not believe what I saw: It was the new French teacher, dressed in a pink housecoat and a pink feather boa like the classic wrestler Ric Flair. That was how he greeted the class. I remember thinking to myself, "I need to get to know him." During break, I tracked him down and introduced myself. After that, our hallway interactions and conversations became more frequent and natural. As time went on, he became one of my Teacher Friends Forever (TFFs).

—Rob

It can be intimidating to approach a teacher who is amazing at what they do. It can also be easy to feel jealous or insecure around them. Don't be. These teachers are as accomplished as they are because *they love to teach*. Make a point of connecting with great educators as much as you can and learn from them.

Be Supportive

Although you may feel like you are the one who needs all the support, that is not true. We all need to support each other in this profession. Be on the lookout for ways you can show your support. Offer help when you can (such as covering for colleagues who are out), share resources, help with school events, celebrate colleagues' accomplishments, and show your peers appreciation whenever you can.

Maximize Your Mentor

Here are some questions to ask your mentor at this point in the school year:

- What time-saving "hacks" do you have that can help me do [insert aspect of your job] more efficiently?
- Can you tell me which colleague is really good at [insert specific skill]? I'd like to collaborate with them and learn more about it.

Take Care of School-Year You

Edith Eger is a brilliant psychologist and author who often shares lessons gleaned from her heartbreaking experience in the Holocaust. According to her interview on Brené Brown's *Unlocking Us* podcast (Brown, 2021), the choices we face in life are among the greatest gifts we'll ever receive because, ultimately, they determine so much. One of Eger's wise strategies is to "choose in the morning how you want to feel at night" (2018). We've put this strategy to the test multiple times, and guess what? It works. For example, if you know it will be a busy day filled with unending tasks and responsibilities, you may choose in the morning to feel *calm* at night so you can recenter and reset before the next day. Or, if it's a day when you want to lean into work and make significant progress, you may choose to feel *proud* or *accomplished* at the end of the day. Different days require different words, and this strategy allows us to honor the season we are in.

Invest in Your Happiness

Many of us have been conditioned to believe that if we are successful, we will be happy. In *The Happiness Advantage* (2010), Shawn Achor suggests otherwise: He wants us to understand that happiness brings success.

For example, think of a typical student who needs to successfully complete elementary school. Are they happy once they do? Only temporarily, because now they need to successfully complete middle school—and then high school, college, and so on. The goalposts keep moving. In *The Happiness Lab* podcast, Yale professor and podcast host Laurie Santos (2023) talks with guest Tony Hale about how we too often fall victim to what psychologists call the *arrival fallacy*—"the idea that when we reach a certain milestone we will find permanent happiness and fulfillment." A similar concept is the *hedonic treadmill*, which refers to people's tendency to return to their baseline level of happiness after a positive or negative event, regardless of what that event is.

Not only does success not bring happiness, but the reverse is closer to the truth: *Happiness brings success*. In other words, when we understand that happiness is an "inside job" and it's up to us to recognize what we can positively influence and to discern our next right thing, we can create permanent positive change.

Happiness isn't just about feeling good; it's about performing well, too. Here's a quick exercise that should drive this point home in your own life. Think of someone at your school whom you would describe as happy—they make you feel good, they share positive energy, and they tend to have a positive influence on others. Write their name here: ____________________

When you think of this person, do you notice a positive correlation among their energy level, productivity, and creativity? Of course you do. According to data Rob shares in his book *STRIVE for Happiness in Education* (Dunlop, 2020), happy people are 31 percent more productive, have 23 percent more energy, and are three times more creative than those who are unhappy. In other words, if you could increase your productivity, energy, and creativity, your success would be likely to grow.

Taking care of yourself and your happiness isn't just a nice thing to do; it's imperative for success in an others-oriented profession like teaching. So if you want to be successful (and we know you do), prioritize your happiness now!

CHAPTER 3 CHECKLIST

This chapter hopefully has you thinking about how to sustain momentum by building relationships with students, parents, and school staff. At this point in the year, it's imperative to stay positive and use the supports that you have access to.

Happiness and Success for Your Students and Classroom

- ☐ Have a few go-to positivity pauses ready to use.
- ☐ Create an interest inventory to get to know students better.
- ☐ Make a list of students you want to try to connect with outside the classroom.
- ☐ Envision questions for a classroom audit and create a survey for students to complete.
- ☐ Think about some challenging students you have. Do you have a "magic ratio" with them?
- ☐ Consider opportunities for student leadership in your classroom.
- ☐ Try some strategies to capture students' attention and see how your students respond.
- ☐ Choose a classroom expectation you want to prioritize by reinforcing with positive praise.
- ☐ Consider what kind of incentive system could work with your students.
- ☐ Come up with ideas for students to recognize peers.
- ☐ List three to five things that students can do when they are finished with a task.
- ☐ Identify your primary will driver as well as those of your three most reluctant students.
- ☐ Consider whether you are communicating with families enough and in the best format. Can you be more efficient and effective with your communications?

- ☐ If you have an upcoming parent-teacher conference, write an outline to follow during your conversation.
- ☐ Consider which aspects of your teaching you want students to assess on a teacher report card.
- ☐ Consider questions to ask students or parents that could help you refine your practice.
- ☐ Ask your mentor any questions that you need answered at this time in the school year.

✓

Happiness and Success for You

- ☐ Reflect on your work-life balance and consider whether you need to make adjustments.
- ☐ Notice and honor bids for connection from your students and colleagues.
- ☐ Prioritize moments to connect with your colleagues.
- ☐ Choose one word that can help anchor you throughout the day.
- ☐ Recognize the connection between happiness and success and consider what you can do to prioritize your happiness to support your success as a teacher.

✓

CHAPTER

Instructional Routines Are Established!

Maximizing Your Teaching Time

As educator and author Lauren M. Kaufman (2025) says, "At the end of the day, engagement isn't about keeping learners busy. It's about keeping them thinking" (para. 30). Effective instruction is a blend of art and science based on not just the quality of the content we are delivering but also the way in which we deliver it. Finding a structure for your lessons that works for you and your students can improve engagement, deepen learning, and contribute to a better classroom community. Though specifics will vary based on your students and the grade you teach, we recommend using the following basic structure:

1. Capture students' attention.
2. Deliver the lesson.
3. Wrap up the lesson.

Capture Students' Attention

Your goal as a teacher is to try to quickly secure your students' attention so you can deliver the content you want them to know before they disengage from the lesson you have thoughtfully planned. Aim to find creative and fun ways to engage students in the lesson right away to connect them to the learning that will take place in the lesson. Here are some strategies to accomplish this:

- Ask a thought-provoking question (e.g., "What would life be like without gravity?").
- Share a surprising fact (e.g., "Did you know octopuses have three hearts?").
- Share a relevant video clip, meme, or story.
- Have students play a quick game or challenge.
- Conduct a hands-on demonstration.
- Present students with a controversial statement or debate prompt.
- Have students answer a brain teaser or riddle related to the topic.
- Ask students to role-play a scenario that puts them in a real-world context.
- Share a personal story or anecdote.
- Discuss an ethical dilemma and ask students what they would do in that situation.
- Have students engage in a quick drawing challenge.
- Play a word association game with students.

In addition to capturing students' attention, these ideas are intended to serve as a springboard into the learning. They can also be an effective way to review learning from a prior lesson or unit. Often students benefit from being told information multiple times and in multiple ways, so when you are brainstorming ways to capture your students' attention, consider what you have previously taught as well as what is next in your instructional plan.

Take note of which attention-getting strategies students like the most. Over time, you will figure out what types of activities work best for your class. Once you do, you will have some go-to hooks that are easy to implement and that you know will grab students' attention.

Deliver the Lesson

Your next step is to build on the momentum of your initial attention-getting strategy and teach the content. When introducing the learning goals for the lesson, be mindful not to talk for too long and lose students' attention. Here are some tips to help you keep students engaged and wanting more during a lesson:

- Involve students by asking them questions rather than just talking at them.
- Use visuals and real-world examples that students can connect to.
- Incorporate storytelling to make the content relatable.
- Have students do a Think-Pair-Share exercise before answering questions in front of the class.
- Use interactive technology both to engage students and to capture their learning.
- Break students into small groups for discussions or to complete problem-solving tasks.
- Set up stations or learning centers for different aspects of the lesson or topic.
- Have students role-play scenarios to reinforce concepts.
- Implement activities that allow students to move around the room (e.g., writing on chart paper or whiteboards stationed in different areas).
- Ask students to complete independent activities (e.g., a writing task, a problem-solving exercise).

Not only will these activities help solidify students' learning, but they will also give *you* a break from presenting at the front of the class and an opportunity to assess student learning through observations and conversations. Look for the sweet spot in terms of time: not enough, and students won't be able to finish what they're doing; too much, and they might drift off task.

Setting a timer that students can see is a great way to keep them focused and on task during a lesson. Following are some other important considerations to keep in mind as you execute your lessons:

1. **Pace yourself.** Be aware of the time and whether you are meeting the goals for the lesson. Do your best to find that happy medium between rushing through things and being left with too much extra time. Before conducting the lesson, try to gauge how much time each part of it should take.
2. **Consider movement and transitions.** When planning your lesson, think of how long students will be sitting in one place. Try to mix in

activities that allow them to move and socialize. This will help them focus and stay engaged in learning.

3. **Anticipate student responses.** Try to anticipate where your students will experience confusion or success. This will help you plan, possibly adding more examples, practice, or discussion. It will also help with your overall pacing and will likely become something you start to do naturally as you build relationships with your students.
4. **Modify and adjust.** Read the room. You are working with human beings and can't always anticipate how they will respond to what you've planned. If students look lost, slow down and reteach. If they find things too easy, use your professional judgment to skip some examples or extend their learning with a challenge.
5. **Model happiness.** Find ways to bring some humor and joy into the room. Students learn best when they feel their best.
6. **Contour lessons to your class.** Use your knowledge of students' home lives, cultures, and interests to plan lessons that are customized to their unique strengths and needs.

You can use the template in Figure 4.1 to ensure you address all the essential elements of a successful lesson.

LESSONS LEARNED

Fix your face! There will be certain lessons or units that you will *love* teaching, and others you are much less passionate about. Regardless of how you feel on the inside, make sure you display interest and enthusiasm to students. No matter their age, they can identify the way their teacher feels about a given topic. To reach as many students as possible, be sure your face conveys a positive attitude toward the lesson.

—Suzanne

Wrap Up the Lesson

Watch your time carefully to avoid an awkward end to the lesson, and give yourself enough time to bring students back together as a whole class

FIGURE 4.1 **General Lesson Plan Template**

<table>
<tr><td colspan="2">Learning Objectives/Success Criteria: What do I want my students to learn and/or be able to do? (These should be specific, measurable, and observable.)</td></tr>
<tr><td colspan="2"></td></tr>
<tr><td colspan="2">Standards: What national/state/district standards are being addressed?</td></tr>
<tr><td colspan="2"></td></tr>
<tr><td colspan="2">Materials: What do I need to teach effectively?</td></tr>
<tr><td>Teacher</td><td>Students</td></tr>
</table>

<table>
<tr><td>Lesson Introduction: How will I engage my students and retrieve their prior learning/background knowledge?</td><td>Pacing</td></tr>
<tr><td></td><td>___ min.</td></tr>
<tr><td colspan="2">Instructional Procedures (if direct instruction is used)</td></tr>
<tr><td>1. Teacher Modeling: Teacher states learning objectives and success criteria and models skills.</td><td>___ min.</td></tr>
<tr><td>2. Guided Practice/Check for Understanding: Responsibility is gradually released to students, who actively practice new learning with teacher.</td><td>___ min.</td></tr>
<tr><td>3. Independent Practice: Students apply new learning independently/ receive differentiated support if needed.</td><td>___ min.</td></tr>
<tr><td colspan="2">Closure: How will I return to the learning objective and determine student understanding?</td></tr>
<tr><td></td><td>___ min.</td></tr>
<tr><td colspan="2">Assessment: What formal or informal data/evidence will I gather to assess students' level of understanding?</td></tr>
<tr><td colspan="2"></td></tr>
<tr><td colspan="2">Intentional Planning Considerations: Differentiation, proactive behavior strategies, scaffolding for MLs, SDIs/504 accommodations/alignment to IEP goals, transitions between lesson activities.</td></tr>
<tr><td colspan="2"></td></tr>
<tr><td colspan="2">Reflective Practice: Teacher and student strengths and areas of growth; consider next instructional steps.</td></tr>
<tr><td colspan="2"></td></tr>
</table>

if they have been broken into groups. To help students consolidate their learning at the end of the lesson, consider these ideas:

- Ask students to recap their most important takeaways about learning aloud or on paper. This will give you insight into what your next lesson should cover.
- Do a know/show activity: On chart paper, a screen, or a whiteboard, write, "I know [learning goal]" on the left and have students show their learning on the right. For example, the statement on the left might read, "I know the steps of the water cycle." On the right, students could draw or label the steps of the water cycle or write a few sentences explaining the steps to show their level of understanding.
- Connect the content to students' lives so that it's meaningful to them. For example, ask, "Why is it important to know how to find the percentage of a number?" This would give students the opportunity to connect this skill to real-life interests or tasks, such as shopping, taxes, or sports statistics.
- Ask students to give a thumbs-up or thumbs-down to check their understanding and gauge their confidence in reaching the learning goal.
- Share a thought-provoking question or problem students can think about for the next lesson.
- Have students complete an exit ticket (e.g., saying what they learned, asking one question they still have, providing a three-word summary).

Whoever Is Doing the Talking Is Doing the Learning

In her 2023 book *Teach for Authentic Engagement,* Lauren Porosoff reminds us that "when students are engaged, their academic achievement improves" (p. 3). If we had to lean into just one low-prep, high-impact instructional strategy to help keep students engaged, it would be providing them with opportunities to respond. Cuticelli and colleagues (2016) define opportunities to respond as "a teaching strategy that elicits student responses by posing questions or comments that provide students with multiple occasions to answer."

Anita Archer is the guru of intentionally planning opportunities to respond. As she says in an instructional video, "Learning is not a spectator sport. We have to get kids involved in their learning. Instruction must be interactive" (Archer, 2015). Later in the video, she explains what she means by interactive instruction: "I say something, you say something; I do something, you do something; I write something, you write something. What it can't be is: I say something, I say something, I say something, I say something, see you tomorrow."

Reflect on one of your recent lessons. How much of it was devoted to you talking rather than students talking? You might be cringing at the realization that you usually do most of the talking. That makes sense sometimes, but often it doesn't. Whoever is talking (or writing, or reading, or responding) is doing the learning. This is why it's so important to provide students with frequent opportunities to respond. Meaningful opportunities to respond require three things: First, you need to do your best to involve *all* students, providing opportunities for everyone to contribute. Second, to do this effectively, you need to require *overt* responses, so that students are saying, writing, or doing something to actively participate. Finally, it's important to structure the process by teaching students the routines and expectations for responding. For example, if you want students to respond chorally, you'd teach them that when you put both of your hands out and pause, that's their cue to respond as a group. If you're asking a multiple-choice question with options *A, B, C,* and *D* as answers, students would know that raising one finger represents choice *A,* two fingers represent choice *B,* and so on. When students know the routines and expectations, you can maintain a perky pace and maximize your instructional minutes.

According to research published in the *Journal of Behavioral Education,* for every minute of instruction, we should aim for three to five simple responses (e.g., responding orally, holding up a response card, nodding to show agreement) and one more complex response (e.g., turn-and-talks, writing something down) (MacSuga-Gage & Gage, 2015). This may sound overwhelming, and it's OK to not work at that brisk a pace all the time, but it is important to bear this research in mind. One of Anita Archer's best-known quotes is "Avoid the void, for they will fill it" (Hurst, 2022). Isn't that brilliant? When there is unstructured time in our classrooms, behavioral issues begin to appear. By constantly inviting students to overtly engage in their learning through opportunities to respond, we minimize this risk.

Help Your Students Retain What They Learn

You've taught the thing. You've tested the thing. A month later, you reference said thing to a sea of blank stares. It happens to the best of us.

Did you know that there is something called the "forgetting curve" (see Figure 4.2)? According to German psychologist Hermann Ebbinghaus (1885/1913), information is lost over time when there is no attempt to retain it.

What does the graph in Figure 4.2 tell us? Our students aren't forgetting things to frustrate their teachers; they're forgetting because their brains are hardwired to only retain the information they find most important, which is the information they consistently interact with. For example, if we were to ask you what you had for dinner last Tuesday, you probably couldn't answer immediately. That's because your brain is doing exactly what it's designed to do: hang on to the information that it needs to keep you safe and alive and that it deems important, discarding the rest. It knows you don't need to store what you had for dinner last Tuesday in your long-term memory. When we sleep, it's almost like a little Zamboni goes through our brains, clearing out what we don't need to survive in the long term.

What does this mean for us as teachers? It's easy for students to forget a lot of what we teach them! According to Anita Archer (2023), we should purposely plan for our students to *retrieve* prior learning and *respond* through writing or speaking so they will *retain* the information. Following are some strategies you can use to help students retrieve information that they may have forgotten so it sticks in their long-term memory.

Hold Throwback Thursdays or Memory Mondays

Ideally, retrieval should be naturally interwoven throughout your instruction. One low-stakes starting point is to incorporate "Throwback Thursdays" or "Memory Mondays" into students' weekly routines, purposefully setting a time when you can ask them questions from a previous unit or invite them to compare new learning with something they previously learned.

FIGURE 4.2 **The Forgetting Curve**

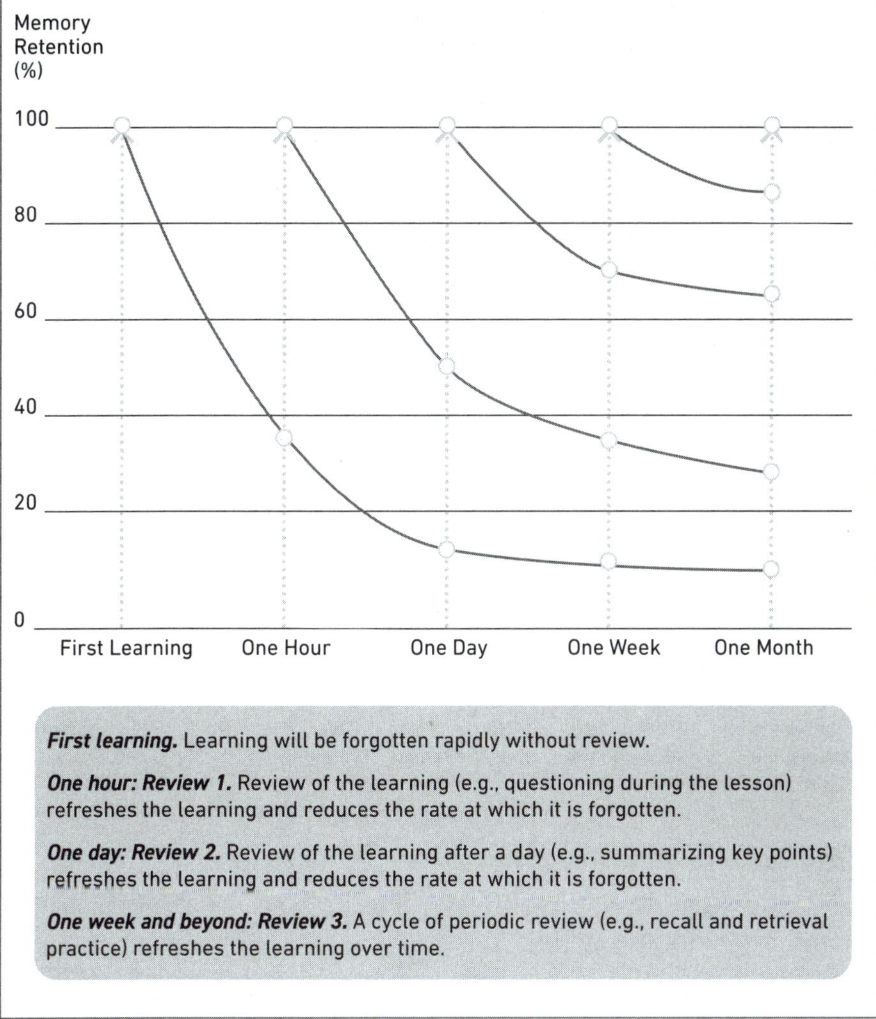

Use Retrieval Grids

Figures 4.3 and 4.4 show retrieval grids for elementary and secondary school. The content of the prompts comes from the first two units of a reading/phonics program and reflects skill sets ranging from rhyming to decoding and comprehension. Some teachers use retrieval grids as a part of their morning meeting, closing circle, or advisory period. Retrieval grids can work well in many contexts. One way is in small groups, in which one student is appointed the scorekeeper. Students take turns choosing a question from the grid for all group members to answer, and then the student

FIGURE 4.3 **Sample Elementary Retrieval Grid**

Read and spell the words: **in** **was** [1 point]	Use the word **gill** in a sentence. [2 points]	What is a way a **neighbor** can help another **neighbor**? [3 points]	Name a **consonant** and its **sound**. [4 points]	Mark the vowel and read the word: **van** [5 points]
Mark the vowel and read the word: **sad** [5 points]	Read and spell the words: **he** **the** [1 point]	What is a **pattern**? [2 points]	How does a tadpole **grow** and **change**? [3 points]	Name a **vowel** and its **sound**. [4 points]
How do **pictures** help a reader under-stand the story? [4 points]	Mark the vowel and read the word: ***gad** [5 points]	Read and spell the words: **they** **with** [1 point]	Show on your face: **happy, sad, surprised, angry** [2 points]	Name three things in a **neighborhood.** [3 points]
What are two **signs** you would see in a **neighborhood**? [3 points]	Name a word that **rhymes** with **bell**. [4 points]	Mark the vowel and read the word: **lab** [5 points]	Read and spell the words: **at** **have** [1 point]	Which is the **adjective**? boy run kind [2 points]
What is the **setting** in a story? [2 points]	How does a seed **change** into a plant? [3 points]	Name a word that **rhymes** with **hat**. [4 points]	Mark the vowel and read the word: ***zin** [5 points]	Read and spell the words: **be** **it** [1 point]

who chose the question shares their answer. The scorekeeper checks the key for the correct response, and all students who got it are awarded points.

As you can see, there is a range of point values in the retrieval grids. The longer ago students learned the content, the more points they receive for a correct answer. For example, say it's February and you're teaching the fourth unit in your course of study. If you were to make a retrieval grid of items from Units 1, 2, and 3, answers to questions from Unit 1 would be worth more points than those from Unit 3 because the retrieval of information learned longer ago is more of a challenge. That's the brilliance of this strategy: It honors the cognitive lift required for students to retrieve past learning.

FIGURE 4.4 **Sample Secondary Retrieval Grid**

Identify one theme from: "The Most Dangerous Game" [5 points]	**Circle the onomatopoeia.** The snake rattled down the dirt road. [1 point]	**Simile or metaphor?** The slinking robber was as quiet as a mouse. [2 points]	**Personification or anthropo-morphism?** The wind slapped me. [3 points]	**Alliteration, assonance, or consonance?** Mike lacks the skills. [4 points]
Alliteration, assonance, or consonance? Let's meet the gleeful beekeper! [4 points]	**Identify one theme from:** *The Outsiders* [5 points]	**Circle the onomatopoeia.** Crack! The lightning hit the tree in the front yard. [1 point]	**Simile or metaphor?** The football player was a tank on the field tonight. [2 points]	**Personification or anthropo-morphism?** Bluey [3 points]
Personification or anthropo-morphism? SpongeBob SquarePants [3 points]	**Alliteration, assonance, or consonance?** Tom took the truck to town. [4 points]	**Identify one theme from:** "The Scarlet Ibis" [5 points]	**Circle the onomatopoeia.** As the tires screeched, I knew an accident was coming. [1 point]	**Simile or metaphor?** Her anger erupted like a volcano. [2 points]
Simile or metaphor? You ain't nothin' but a hound dog, cryin' all the time. [2 points]	**Personification or anthropo-morphism?** Dancing leaves [3 points]	**Alliteration, assonance, or consonance?** Sally tells Billy the lizard is ill. [4 points]	**Identify one theme from:** "The Cask of Amontillado" [5 points]	**Circle the onomatopoeia.** The heavy rain plopped down into puddles in the driveway. [1 point]
Circle the onomatopoeia. The wind was howling in the darkness. [1 point]	**Simile or metaphor?** You are my sunshine. [2 points]	**Personification or anthropo-morphism?** Charlotte from *Charlotte's Web* [3 points]	**Alliteration, assonance, or consonance?** Dan stamped Sam's hand. [4 points]	**Identify one theme from:** *A Christmas Carol* [5 points]

Source: Courtesy of Nicole Brandecker. Adapted with permission.

Have Students Do a Brain Dump

A brain dump is exactly what it sounds like. Pause what you're doing, set a timer, and tell students to write down or discuss in pairs everything they remember about a topic they previously learned.

Provide Feedback That Moves Students Forward

As Rick Wormeli (2012) says, "Students can learn without our grades, but they can't learn without feedback" (para. 4). However, not all feedback is created equal.

Here's an exercise to prove this point. In the box below, write at least six words or phrases you would typically use as feedback on student work:

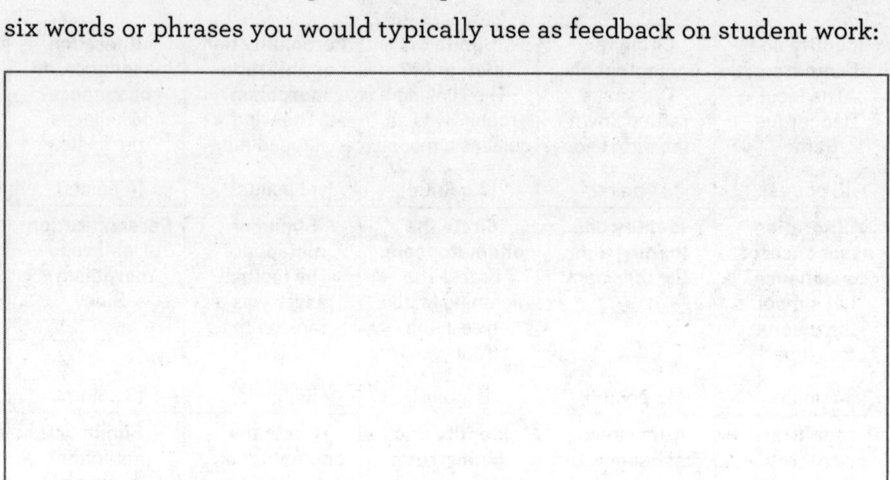

Now pretend you're playing basketball with a friend who happens to be blindfolded. They do their best and launch the ball at the hoop, but they miss. Not to worry, though, because you will give them feedback to help.

But here's the catch: You can only use what you wrote in the box above.

How did you do? You may have recorded examples of specific feedback, but we would venture to guess that you more likely wrote things like "Great effort!" or "Awesome job!" or "Add more detail!" (ha!). Clearly, those phrases aren't going to help your friend meet their goal of getting the ball in the hoop.

This exercise shows that generic feedback doesn't help students reach their learning goal. The language isn't specific enough and fails to overtly tell students where they are in relation to the goal and what they need to do to get closer to it. Targeted feedback sounds like, "Move a little to the left and then throw it" or "You are about 10 inches short. Try adding some power, but throw the ball in the exact same place." See how different that sounds? You moved from low-quality, generic feedback to higher-quality, specific feedback that will help your friend meet their goal.

In their 2022 *Educational Leadership* article "Getting GREAT at Feedback," Fisher and Frey offer the acronym GREAT as a way to remember what they consider to be the dimensions of strong feedback for students: *growth-oriented*, *real*, *empathetic*, *asked-for*, and *timely*:

- **Growth-oriented:** The feedback is constructive rather than critical. For example: "You are off to a great start. Here's how adding detail to this part in your writing can help your reader understand why this was such an important moment in your life."
- **Real:** The feedback is honest, targeted, and actionable and helps the student understand what to stop, start, or change. For example: "This part of your writing could confuse your reader. I know this was a really special time for you, but this part makes it seem like it was an ordinary day. How could you adjust your language to show that this was an exciting time?"
- **Empathetic:** The feedback balances critique and care. For example: "I know it can be really difficult to paint a picture for a reader who isn't familiar with this experience when it is so easily visualized in your head. Including some descriptive details may make it a bit easier."
- **Asked-for:** The feedback encourages dialogue with the student by providing an opportunity for them to ask questions or seek clarification. For example: "What questions do you have about adding specific detail to this part of your writing?"
- **Timely:** The feedback is delivered soon after the work is completed.

Simply put, your feedback should be adjusted based on the student's needs, their relation to the learning goal, and the task at hand. New teachers' bandwidth is limited. Therefore, it's important to spend your finite time, effort, and energy on the things that move the dial by bringing students closer to their learning goal. This may require more than just writing "Great job!" on an assignment. Proactively providing timely, high-quality feedback will increase student independence and success over time.

Make Sure to Teach More Than You Assign

To ensure balanced instruction, we need to reflect on how much we are *teaching* versus how much we are *assigning*. Our job is not just to keep students occupied, but to explicitly teach concepts in a way that deepens student learning and builds their confidence. So, when planning lessons, always ask yourself, "Am I teaching or assigning?"

LESSONS LEARNED

A new 5th grade teacher reached out to express that she was overwhelmed with planning. She said she was staying after school until 7:00 each night planning for the next day. During our discussion, I realized that her planning mainly involved searching online for activities for students to do in class. This was taking an incredible amount of time. What's more, she had to collect and assess this work during class to keep students on task.

To ease the burden, I helped her plan a cross-curricular unit that had students create a website on an endangered animal of their choice. To start, we had each student find the best endangered animal website they could. As a class, we then selected one site to use as a model for the ones students would create. Then, we analyzed the factors that made the website we chose so effective and developed success criteria for students' websites. With the criteria as a guide, we taught a series of mini-lessons that took students from research to the final product.

At one point, I asked the teacher to walk around the room and tell me what she thought students needed to work on next. She found that they needed to learn how to capitalize titles, and I agreed. Her initial idea was to find a handout online to practice capitalization. Instead, we had students analyze titles on the model website and create capitalization rules based on those titles.

Later, the teacher told me how much more engaged her students were and how much more they were learning from this assignment compared with others. Instead of simply reading and answering questions on a worksheet, they were actively researching, designing, and learning a new skill: website design. The teacher also commented that she was no longer staying at school until 7:00 p.m. and that assigning a project like this was much easier and more rewarding to her as a teacher than having to assign a lot of smaller assignments.

—Rob

LESSONS LEARNED

A new 3rd grade teacher, frustrated that her students weren't applying the writing skills she was teaching, asked me for help. "I show them a metaphor in a published book, but they aren't ending up in their writing," she said. "We've been working on figurative language, and they can do it on worksheets, but it's rare to find examples in their personal narratives."

After talking through lesson plans with her and conducting some observations, I realized that this teacher was assigning much more than she was teaching. She had her students complete worksheets identifying figurative language, but she wasn't teaching them how to incorporate what they learned in their writing.

I encouraged the teacher to create her own working draft of a personal narrative and use it to model adding figurative language. Explicitly showing students how to transfer their skills into drafts helped them understand how to do it themselves.

—Suzanne

Practice Intentional Instruction

You may notice that there never seems to be enough time to get through everything you need to in a lesson. Being intentional with our time is vital to our effectiveness as teachers and overall happiness as human beings. Are you using your time to build new learning or just keep kids busy? *Teaching* is an active process that involves breaking down concepts, modeling strategies, checking for understanding, and guiding students through practice before we can expect them to complete tasks independently. *Assigning*, by contrast, is passive, placing the burden of learning on the student without providing enough scaffolding to ensure success.

Some elementary teachers ask students to write journal entries about their weekends on Mondays. Without explicit instruction or success criteria, this kind of assignment could be considered busywork. However, if you model writing your own entries and complete think-alouds to highlight mechanics like capitalization, proper spacing, and punctuation, the task becomes an extension of learning rather than an isolated assignment.

To take a secondary school example, consider an assignment that asks students to create a podcast. It is not enough merely to show students how to use the technology and give them time to work on the task. There are so many aspects of recording a podcast that the teacher needs to unpack for students, such as purpose and audience, research, episode structure, recording and editing techniques, and so on. Analyzing sample podcasts together and guiding students through each step of the process sets them up for learning and successful completion of the assignment.

LESSONS LEARNED

During the COVID-19 pandemic, I was one of the technology coaches supporting our teachers. Remote teaching was new to everyone, and we were all trying to figure it out together. One thing I noticed was a shift to more assigning and less teaching. It was difficult to teach through a screen, so instead, many teachers gravitated to posting assignments. As the remote learning continued, ungraded assignments began to pile up for teachers, causing them a lot of stress. It became clear that although assigning may have been easier than teaching, keeping up with assessments became much more difficult.

—Rob

Differentiate Your Teaching

The art and science of teaching often come together when we find strategies to meet students where they are. Most classrooms reflect a variety of backgrounds, cultures, and academic and social needs, as well as a variety of learning preferences. Some students will have specific differentiation approaches outlined in their individualized education or 504 plans, but it's important to differentiate for *all* students. When you are planning lessons or units, keep your students' learning profiles at the forefront of your mind so that they continue to make progress under your care.

Differentiation can be time-consuming, especially for new teachers who may not have a toolbox filled with go-to strategies and resources at this point in their career. But differentiation is less a set of strategies than a way of thinking about teaching and learning. When considering sustainable differentiation in the classroom, be sure to focus on these four areas:

- **Content:** *What* students will learn
- **Process:** *How* and *when* students will master the content
- **Product:** *How* students demonstrate that they've learned the content
- **Learning environment:** *Where* students learn and complete their work

Pause here to reflect on these areas. Read the prompts in Figure 4.5, and consider having students respond to them. How might these areas of differentiation influence your planning to make learning meaningful to all students?

FIGURE 4.5 **Learning Preferences**

What is the skill you are trying to learn? (Content)
How and when do you want to learn it? (Process)
How do you want to show that you learned it? (Product)
Where would you like to learn it? (Learning environment)

Here are some strategies you can use to plan and implement effective and sustainable differentiation for each of the four focus areas:

Content

- Provide students with the following options:
  - — Texts at different readability levels
  - — Audio and/or video versions of text
  - — Vocabulary and/or spelling lists
- Preteach concepts to build background knowledge.
- Extend concepts to deepen understanding.
- Offer varying levels of support, complexity, and challenge.

Process

- Break students into small groups to reteach content and/or extend concepts.
- Provide manipulatives and hands-on learning support.
- Adjust pacing.
- Adjust timelines for assignments.
- Incorporate information from student interest surveys (see Chapter 3) into lessons.
- Provide students with word banks and/or graphic organizers.
- Have students work independently, in pairs, in small groups, or as a whole class, depending on what works best for them.

Product

- Include both written and project-based assessments.
- Provide rubrics tailored to students' various skill levels and expectations.
- Accept both typed and handwritten work.

Learning Environment

- Allow students to choose their preferred workspaces.
- Implement systems and structures that make it easy for students to receive support from teachers and classmates.

Use a Question Matrix

Take a look at the question matrix in Figure 4.6 and jot down what you notice.

FIGURE 4.6 **Sample Question Matrix**

Set 1

What is . . . ?	When/where is . . . ?	Which is . . . ?
What did . . . ?	When/where did . . . ?	Which did . . . ?
What can . . . ?	When/where can . . . ?	Which can . . . ?

Set 2

Who is . . . ?	Why is . . . ?	How is . . . ?
Who did . . . ?	Why did . . . ?	How did . . . ?
Who can . . . ?	Why can . . . ?	How can . . . ?

Set 3

What would . . . ?	Where/when would . . . ?	Which would . . . ?
What will . . . ?	Where/when will . . . ?	Which will . . . ?
What might . . . ?	Where/when might . . . ?	Which might . . .

Set 4

Who would . . . ?	Why would . . . ?	How would . . . ?
Who will . . . ?	Why will . . . ?	How will . . . ?
Who might . . . ?	Why might . . . ?	How might . . . ?

We hope you noticed that the question stems in sets 1 and 2 generate *explicit*, right-there questions that usually have only one correct answer, while the ones in sets 3 and 4 generate *implicit* questions with multiple possible correct responses. (Although this book is printed in black and white, in a traditional question matrix, each quadrant uses a different font color.) You can use this tool yourself to create meaningful questions that require different types of thinking for formative or summative assessment, or to help *students* create meaningful questions to ask and answer when reviewing their learning. For example, students can pair up, roll a die onto a printout of the matrix, and use the prompt the die lands on to create a question for the other student to answer. Another option is for students to work individually to create and answer questions with your direction (e.g., "Ryan, you will create and answer one question from the red quadrant and one from the blue quadrant. Lauren, you'll do the same for the green and purple." (Note: If you tell your students you'll be using the questions they come up with on an upcoming test, you will likely find that they create sophisticated, challenging questions. This means they are digging deeper into the content to try to "stump" their classmates—a win-win!) You can even ask parents to use the question matrix to ask their child questions about school and gain a better understanding of what they are learning.

As Carol Ann Tomlinson says in *How to Differentiate Instruction in Academically Diverse Classrooms* (2017), "The goal when differentiating content is to offer approaches to 'input' (information, ideas, and skills) that meet students individually where they are" (p. 132). In other words, you can't make things relevant for students or expect rigor from them if you don't *know* them. Begin where your students are, consider which focus area may help them most, and start there. This will get *all* your students closer to reaching their learning goals.

Integrate Technology in Meaningful Ways

One good thing about being a new teacher is that you probably already have at least some comfort with technology. As you kick off your teaching career, look for ways to use technology to truly enhance student learning. In other words, instead of thinking, "This app is really cool, let's see how I can use it," start with the content first. Here are some questions to consider when planning to introduce new tech tools in your class:

- Does this technology support student learning goals?
- Does it help students engage more deeply with the content?
- Is this the best way to teach this concept, or am I using technology just because it is available?

Students need to see technology in the classroom as a tool for learning. At home, students usually use tech to relax, have fun, and pass the time. Explain to them that in class, these tools are intended to support their learning, that it's a privilege to use them, and that they must always be used appropriately. Explicitly show them how to use the technology and set clear expectations for using it. Make it clear to students that if they are not using these tools effectively, they will be provided with an alternative way of learning. If you are too lenient with your expectations around technology, it can quickly become more of a nuisance than a beneficial learning tool.

LESSONS LEARNED

This year, a new 1st grade teacher asked me to help her with educational technology. She was effectively using tablets for phonics practice, but she had noticed that students would sometimes use the tablets when they weren't supposed to. Some students would quietly slip them out of their chair pockets, log on, and play on apps that weren't a part of the phonics program.

All we needed to do to address this situation was change how students accessed the technology. Instead of storing them in chair pockets, we put them all in one place so that the teacher would notice when they were being accessed. This helped reduce students' temptation to use the tablets inappropriately and ensured that they were only used as instructional tools.

—Suzanne

Use Technology to Promote Active Learning

Most students *consume* technology all the time, but as educators, we want them to *actively engage* with it. Here are some ways students can use technology for the purpose of active learning:

- Blogging and creating digital portfolios
- Engaging in gamified learning
- Publishing written work using online design apps (e.g., Canva) to make the work more visually appealing
- Creating videos, podcasts, or websites
- Coding and designing digital games
- Collaborating with peers on digital work
- Engaging with interactive simulations

Consider the SAMR Model

Districts and schools invest a lot of their budget into providing and supporting technology, so it is important that we use it to provide learning opportunities with added value. A great model to ensure this is the Substitution, Augmentation, Modification, Redefinition (SAMR) model (Puentedura, 2013). Here's how the model breaks down:

- **Substitution:** This is when you use technology as a direct replacement for traditional tools (e.g., using a digital worksheet instead of a hard copy). There is no functional change in the way the activity works.
- **Augmentation:** This is similar to substitution, but in this case technology adds a functional benefit to the assignment (e.g., collaborating with peers in real time on an online document). The task could be completed without technology, but the digital tool enhances students' learning experience.
- **Modification:** This is when you significantly redesign the learning task using technology to enhance engagement and interactivity (e.g., having students create podcasts instead of delivering oral presentations). The task is significantly altered to give students a much different experience than they would get without technology.
- **Redefinition:** When you redefine a task using technology, you provide new learning opportunities that would not be possible without it (e.g., using virtual reality to explore historical sites). Here, the task becomes something that can only be done using technology.

Augmentation and modification *enhance* the task, whereas modification and redefinition *transform* it. Your goal is to ensure that any tasks using technology fall into the augmentation, modification, or redefinition category rather than the substitution category so that students can get the most value out of the tools.

Embrace AI in Education

Although artificial intelligence (AI) has been part of education since the 1960s, only recently have both educators and students gained widespread access to AI for nearly every task. It isn't going away—in fact, it's only becoming more powerful and more deeply integrated into everyday learning. As Jon Kabat-Zinn (1994) wisely says, "You can't stop the waves, but you can learn to surf." Rather than resist AI, explore how you can use it to support your teaching and help prepare students for the future. A good starting point is simply to play around with it to learn more about the capabilities of this technology. The more you play with AI, the more you will find ways to meaningfully connect it to instruction—and the more you understand it, the better able you'll be to use it successfully with students.

With older students especially, this provides an opening to discuss issues related to the use of AI—for example, when it's OK to use and when it's not, how to build digital citizenship skills, and the importance of evaluating AI-generated content for accuracy and authenticity. As edtech expert Monica Burns (2024) notes, you can also guide students to "evaluate their own choices as they participate in digital spaces, including the impact of sharing AI-generated content without proper attribution" (pp. 52–53).

LESSONS LEARNED

I was struggling to get many of my students to understand where to separate their written text into paragraphs. So armed with information I had collected in a student interest survey at the beginning of the year, I used AI to generate unbroken passages of text about my students' favorite shows and tasked them with breaking the passages into paragraphs. Students loved this lesson, and we had an amazing discussion on where to start and end paragraphs. AI enabled me to quickly contour my lesson to students' interests and enhance their learning. Of course, I acknowledged to students that I had used AI to create these written pieces, thereby modeling academic integrity—important to do when using generative AI.

—Rob

Use Technology to Level the Learning Playing Field

As you get to know your students better, consider what kind of technology you can use to support their individual learning needs. Here are a few suggestions:

- **Adaptive learning platforms** that adjust content based on student responses to provide personalized learning paths
- **Assistive technology** such as text-to-speech and speech-to-text programs, closed-captioning, and audiobooks
- **Gamified platforms** that make learning engaging and allow students to progress at their own pace
- **Choice boards** that allow students to choose how they would like to engage in their learning

- **Project- or inquiry-based learning tools** that offer students a comfortable entry point to learning and an engaging way to express their understanding

LESSONS LEARNED

I have a student this year who, owing to a language impairment, is unable to read and write without the support of voice-to-text software. He has been provided with his own computer and trained in how to use assistive technology. He is extremely efficient with this tool and uses it to complete the same assignments that his classmates do. The software enables him to effectively engage with the same content as his peers and to show his understanding. This has made an incredible difference in this student's learning experience. It truly speaks to the power of using technology to level the playing field and support students who need it.

—Rob

Celebrate the Wins

If you spend your energy searching for and ruminating on things that are not going as expected, you will likely struggle to enjoy coming to work each day. However, if you can train your brain to celebrate the wins no matter how big or small, then chances are you will find joy in each day.

LESSONS LEARNED

I had the honor of seeing motivational author Tony Robbins speak several years ago. It was one of the most inspiring events I have ever attended. I left with many takeaways, but one that stuck with me the most was his challenge to "trade expectations for appreciation." This switch of focus can quickly help us find the positives in most situations.

—Rob

Train Your Brain to Focus on the Positive

If you tend to focus on negatives, you may need to train yourself to be more positive. One great way to do this is to practice gratitude. Doing so can enhance neuroplasticity, the brain's ability to adapt and change, by strengthening neural pathways associated with positive emotions and reducing the power of negative emotions (Alexander et al., 2021).

The more we practice focusing on the positive, the more natural it becomes. Practicing gratitude consists of three steps: *recognizing* when something good happens, *recalling* it at the end of the day, and *recording* it somewhere. The key is to explore different ways of incorporating gratitude into our lives every day. Here are some ideas to get started:

- Keep a gratitude journal.
- Go on gratitude walks. During these walks, mindfully focus on noticing and appreciating the positive aspects of your surroundings and your life. This is helpful for students, too: A principal colleague of Suzanne's noted that on days when she took students on a gratitude walk, the number of behavior notices decreased.
- Keep a gratitude jar. Make a practice of writing down things you're grateful for on slips of paper and adding them to the jar. Over time, the jar becomes a visible reminder of positive moments and blessings in your life.
- Use a gratitude app. There are numerous apps designed to support gratitude practice. Recording and reflecting on things you're thankful for each day boosts mindfulness and positive emotions.
- Recite morning affirmations that reflect gratitude.
- Write thank-you notes.
- Meditate or pray with gratitude in mind.

Both of us have been intentionally practicing gratitude for many years. Suzanne writes in her journal each night; Rob uses an app called Happyfeed. It is important to find what works best for you.

LESSONS LEARNED

I have been writing in a gratitude journal since 1997, and it's always the most powerful practice of my day. It encourages me to move through my day on the lookout for the "glimmers"—the good stuff that I'm grateful for—and notice them in real time. When I recall those glimmers at the end of the day and record them in my journal, I signal to my brain that good things have happened in the past, good things are happening in the present, and good things are likely to happen in the future.

—Suzanne

Seek Out Small Wins

We put a lot into designing our lessons and setting our students up to succeed, so it can be very frustrating when students are not getting the concepts or following our expectations. If we just focus on that frustration, we can quickly become mired in negativity. Seeking out small wins throughout the day helps us realize that we are making progress and should be proud of ourselves.

LESSONS LEARNED

At the beginning of this year, I was struggling to believe that I was succeeding with my students. I had a very complex class with an array of academic needs, including 12 students with IEPs, and I feared I was unable to support all the needs in my class. No matter what I did, students were not progressing at the rate I expected.

One day, my sister (and teaching partner) pulled me aside and told me that I needed to find the smaller wins that my students were experiencing and be proud of them. I took her advice and quickly began to feel more successful and proud of both myself and my students.

—Rob

Celebrate Wins with Your Class

It's important to involve your students in celebrating successes. Here are some ideas to consider:

- Kick off each day by celebrating the previous day's wins together. This can be as simple as acknowledging student achievement, sharing moments of gratitude, or allowing students to recognize peers.
- Have daily or weekly rituals such as "shout-outs" or "success circles" to solidify the importance of celebrating wins. Building these into your day or week will increase the likelihood that they will become routine for students.
- Build celebrations into class meetings and community circles. This is a great way to begin or end class on a positive note.
- Celebrate wins in the hallway during breaks to strengthen your relationships with your students.
- Use sticky notes to recognize student success in the moment, writing a quick message to congratulate the student or acknowledge their effort. You can create a space in your classroom to post these, or you can place them in an area where students will find them and get a pleasant surprise (e.g., in their locker or desk).

Celebrate Wins with Your Colleagues

Find a regular time of day that works for you to seek out a colleague and share your best moments. This could be as simple as saying, "Tell me something good" at lunchtime or at the end of the day. If you make this a daily practice, you will train your brain to seek out those wins even on tough days.

Develop relationships with "green-flag" colleagues—those who are good both *to* you and *for* you. (See Chapter 5 for more on green-flag and red-flag colleagues.) Making the intentional choice to surround yourself with other positive educators will help you find more joy throughout the day. Keep an eye out for educators who are always smiling and seem to be trying hard to mine for the good. Even better, *be* that educator!

Maximize Your Mentor

Now that you have welcomed students and established routines and are well into teaching your curriculum, here are some questions to ask your mentor at this point in the school year:

- Can we find a way for you to observe me and provide feedback?
- Can we find a way for me to observe you or another colleague?

Take Care of School-Year You

We delight in the meme depicting Ross from *Friends* with his fingers pressing his eyelids in anguish and disbelief, with the caption "Me trying to figure out what to eat for dinner after making 1,204,389 decisions at school." As teachers, we are constantly making decisions—for our students, our classroom, our family, and ourselves. Teachers are prime candidates for "decision fatigue." According to a piece on the Medical News Today website (Johnson, 2020), decision fatigue is when, "after making many decisions, a person's ability to make additional decisions becomes worse" (para. 1). Johnson goes on to note that "a human's ability to make decisions can get worse after making many decisions, as their brain will be more fatigued" (para. 5) and that "this fatigue applies to all decisions, not just the large or more difficult ones" (para. 6). When we face too many choices, we can experience cognitive overload, which makes us less equipped to handle things presently, patiently, or optimistically.

If we want our brains to feel less fatigued, we have to make fewer decisions. Think about some of the routine decisions you make and consider how you can streamline them. This is a gentle and generous way to take care of our future selves.

LESSONS LEARNED

Every Monday, my dear late friend Corinne would wear the same outfit. "Mondays are hard enough," she'd say. "Why add an outfit decision to it?"

One day, I complimented my buddy Brian on his new brown shoes. "I've got a black pair just like it," he said. "I'm all set."

Corinne and Brian didn't get fatigued by making choices they didn't have to make. By limiting their choices, they minimized their decision making. I was so inspired by Corinne's example that now whatever outfit I wear to church on Sunday doubles as my Monday outfit!

—Suzanne

Do what you can to minimize mundane decision making so you can devote your cognitive energy to the good stuff: doing great things for your students.

CHAPTER 4 CHECKLIST

This chapter hopefully finds you at a point in the year with established classroom routines, able to hone your instruction to make learning meaningful for your students. Take time to reflect on how your lessons are going and look for innovative ways to make things better for both you and your students.

Happiness and Success for Your Students and Classroom

- ☐ Create a list of three to five go-to ways to capture students' attention.
- ☐ Gauge students' relative success with different types of collaborative learning (e.g., pairs, small groups, learning stations).
- ☐ Create a go-to list of three to five no-prep ways for students to consolidate what they've learned at the end of a lesson.
- ☐ Ask your colleagues what they do for retrieval practice.
- ☐ Reflect on your current practice. How many opportunities to respond (simple and complex) do you typically incorporate in each lesson?
- ☐ Reflect on whether you are providing meaningful feedback to your students in a timely manner.
- ☐ Reflect on your latest teaching or an upcoming lesson. Are you assigning more than you're teaching, or teaching more than you're assigning?

- ☐ Reflect on whether you are spending too much time marking work and look for ways to teach more while assessing less.
- ☐ Ask your colleagues if they have strategies for efficiently and sustainably differentiating instruction.
- ☐ Break down how you use technology using the SAMR model and envision how you can use technology more effectively in the classroom.
- ☐ Find out if your district offers software to help differentiate instruction.
- ☐ Incorporate ways to celebrate wins together with students.
- ☐ Make at least one positive phone call home a week.

✓

Happiness and Success for You

- ☐ Celebrate something good with a colleague.
- ☐ Reduce decision fatigue by considering which routine decisions you can streamline or cut.
- ☐ Find a way of practicing gratitude that works best for you and commit to doing it daily.

✓

CHAPTER 5

The Year Is in Full Swing! Maintaining Your Happiness and Success as a Teacher

Our bodies' sensory systems gather *one billion* bits of data per second, but our brains can process only 10 bits per second (Zheng & Meister, 2025). So it's important that we train our brains to be very selective about what to focus on. As educators, it can be all too easy to focus on the negative noise around us. The more we do this, the less likely we are to be happy and have a positive impact on our students. If we allow ourselves to get lost in the noise, our students are not going to receive the best version of us. Ask yourself these questions:

- Am I putting my energy into what matters most for my students right now?
- How might shifting my focus improve both my students' experience and mine?
- What small shift in language, thought, or action could I make today to stay more connected to the needs of my students?
- What negative noise is diverting my attention from enjoying teaching?

You've spent a lot of time working hard to plan lessons, explain concepts, and prepare students for assessments. But when your students look back years from now, it won't be the worksheets, the test scores, or even the specific lessons they'll remember most. What will stick with them is whether they felt seen, heard, and valued in the classroom. They'll remember the encouragement you gave when they struggled, the times you celebrated their growth, and the simple, everyday ways you showed them they mattered. Likewise, the greatest joys in your career will not be perfect tests, high averages, or amazing culminating projects, but the connections that you form with your students.

Strengthen Your Craft

Suzanne's colleague Brian once told her that his second year of teaching was the hardest. Why? "That's when all the support systems came off," he said. "I didn't have an official mentor to bounce ideas off, and new-teacher meetings were done. I had always gotten a lot of good ideas there. Everyone just kind of expected me to have it all figured out on my own. And I didn't."

You may feel a bit like Brian at the end of your first year. As a reflective practitioner, take time to acknowledge your strengths, remember your wins, and identify opportunities for growth as you refine your practice by implementing the following strategies.

Ask Reflective Questions

Teacher and author Anita Brady (2024) invites teachers to ask themselves these four reflective questions:

- **What did I accomplish?** This question forces us to mine for the good and give ourselves credit for the things we've successfully done. Maybe you reached a student who didn't seem reachable at the beginning of the year, or established more positive relationships with colleagues than you thought you would. Whatever it is, celebrate what has gone *right* so far this year!
- **What boundary did I keep?** Were you able to arrive at or leave work at a reasonable time most days? Were you able to block off some time for yourself after school? What did you do to honor both your work *and* yourself?

- **How was I creative?** What have you done to put your own creative twist on an assignment, lesson, or project?
- **What will I continue to do next year?** Sure, you may have had some false starts or lessons that didn't go the way you wanted. But did you figure out an organizational system for files and resources? Did you find an effective tech tool that your students loved? Were you on a committee that helped you feel more connected to your school and colleagues? Consider what has served you or your students well this year that you'd like to continue next year.

The following prompts will help you further reflect on your practice and begin forming some goals going forward:

- Think about two or three wonderful things that have happened so far this year (e.g., a student finally got it, a parent who questioned you at the beginning of the year is now grateful for your work). What is something you can put in place now to *increase* the likelihood of those things happening again in the future?
- Think about two or three challenging things that have happened so far this year (e.g., you blundered a protocol, you had a conflict with a colleague or parent). What is something you can put in place now to *decrease* the likelihood of those things happening again in the future?

Another strategy is to use a goal-setting chart like the one in Figure 5.1. This can help you figure out where to focus your energies after a busy and disorienting year.

Record Yourself Teaching

One of the most effective ways both new and experienced teachers can make meaningful changes is to record themselves teaching. Whether you record just a short block or an entire lesson, watching it afterward will allow you to identify strengths and goal areas. For example, if you watch a video of yourself and notice that you never budge from the front of the room, you might set a goal to move around more. Or if you notice that you're always calling on the same students, you might decide to incorporate strategies to encourage contributions from others.

FIGURE 5.1 **Goal-Setting Chart**

Start: What is something new you want to incorporate in the future?	
Stop: What did you try that didn't work and that you don't want to bring into the next year?	
Continue: What worked? What will you continue next year?	
Consider: What is something you wanted to try but didn't have the capacity or resources to do in the first year?	

Observe a Veteran Teacher

Have you ever heard it said that the best PD is the teacher down the hall? It's a statement that just about every teacher would agree with, no matter how long they have been teaching. If you would like to consult a veteran teacher at your school, we suggest reaching out to your principal to get permission and coverage and then thinking about a colleague to meet with. They should

- Teach the same grade level and/or subject.
- Have students with similar needs to yours.
- Excel at something you want to get better at (e.g., classroom management, organization, student engagement).
- Have a personality that is similar to yours (this is important because if you are more of an introvert, you may not be able to replicate the strategies that are successful for a more extroverted teacher).

Not sure whom to visit? Your principal, mentor, or other colleagues may have some suggestions based on what it is you want to see.

There will be times during your observation when you're bound to say, "Yes! I do that too!" and feel validated, and others when you think, "Huh! I never thought to approach it that way." Here are some things to look for during a collegial observation:

- Classroom management strategies
- Routines and transitions
- Clarity of learning objectives
- Differentiation strategies
- Classroom organization strategies
- Levels of questioning
- Checks for understanding
- Opportunities to respond
- Inclusion practices

Turn Colleagues into Friends

Up until this point in the school year, much of your time and energy has been focused on your students (and rightfully so!). Now is a good time to turn toward your colleagues and consider which ones contribute most to your overall happiness.

Colleagues can fall into three categories: red flags, green flags, and neutral. Most of us are familiar with red-flag colleagues: They are the ones who display toxic traits such as constantly gossiping, talking negatively about their students, and thriving on conflict. Our nervous system feels dysregulated before, during, or after interactions with red-flag colleagues. We feel bad. We feel anxious. We feel uneasy. They are not good to us. They are not good *for* us.

Green-flag colleagues, by contrast, are accepting and nurturing. They make us feel safe and are genuinely happy when we win. We can be fully ourselves around our green-flag people. They are good to us. They are good *for* us. Make an effort to connect with them, as these relationships will help you not only survive but thrive as you progress into the next year and the rest of your career.

LESSONS LEARNED

In my first year, I taught in a large building with more than 100 colleagues. This was wonderful because I could ask so many people for help, but finding "my people" was a bit of a challenge. Still, I managed to find my green-flag colleagues. Twenty years later, some of the people I met in my first year of teaching have become lifelong friends. They are there to celebrate my successes and to support me when things are challenging. Their steady presence *in* school has evolved to become a welcome presence *outside* school, and they are now part of my "family of the heart."

—Suzanne

To find the green-flag people in your school, consider these questions:

- Who makes themselves available when you need something?
- Who consistently shares ideas and resources?
- Who makes you laugh?
- Who is there to give you advice when you ask for it?
- Who checks in on you by doing things like popping into your classroom or sending a quick text?
- Who *finds* time and *makes* time for you?
- Who compliments you when you succeed?

LESSONS LEARNED

One of the things I am most proud of as an educator is the team that I have surrounded myself with. For many years, I have focused on building relationships with educators who not only are enjoyable to be around but also push me to be better at my job.

I use a strategy that I call "random acts of recognition." Essentially, when a positive thought about someone goes through my head, I try to share it with that person immediately in the easiest way possible, whether that means putting a sticky note on their desk, sending them a quick email, or just taking the time to share that thought with them in person. The key is to keep it simple and not overcomplicate it.

One day, I was reading an article that popped up on social media about how to "teach happier." When I was done reading it, I thought, "That was awesome! Who is this person?" It turned out to be Suzanne. I followed her on social media and messaged her to tell her how much I enjoyed her article. We have been supporting each other and collaborating on different projects, such as this book, ever since. Suzanne has truly become an amazing friend and important part of my educational journey—all because I took a couple minutes to thank her for her article.

Too often, we neglect to share positive thoughts about colleagues with them. To find your people more quickly, take the time to openly recognize them and the great work they are doing.

—Rob

As you refine your craft and become more familiar with the structures, systems, and routines of your school and district, you will increase your capacity to develop and strengthen collegial relationships. When you feel like you have the energy, reach out and start forming those relationships.

Establish and Maintain Happy and Healthy Routines at School

As educators, we are fortunate to have relatively consistent and predictable work hours. This makes it easier for us to establish routines and to find a rhythm that serves us best. As you move through the year, take time to think about how you are optimizing the structure of your day to feel happier and healthier.

Determine When You Feel the Best

There are those who bounce out of bed at 5:00 a.m. to work out (Suzanne), and there are those who stay under the covers as long as they can (Rob). There are those who write best during the day (Suzanne) and those who write best after their kids go to bed (Rob). When are you most productive? When are you in the best mood? When do you struggle the most? These are all important things to consider when trying to establish a routine to make you happier and healthier. Here are some examples of routines to consider to enhance your personal well-being:

- If you are a morning person, come in early and get organized for the day. If you are not a morning person, stay later to prepare for tomorrow.
- If your peak hours of focus are from 8:00 to 10:00 a.m., if possible, teach the lessons that require you to be at your best and that you find most challenging to teach within that window.
- If you experience an energy dip at a certain time of day, see if you can plan an activity during that period that requires less of your energy, such as having your students focus on an independent task. (This may be easier for teachers who teach the same group of students throughout the day, but most teachers should be able to do this at least sometimes.)
- If you need a boost to end the day strong, structure some fun into the afternoon that allows you to laugh and connect with students or staff.
- If you have a busy life at home, give yourself time to wind down and recharge after school.

Connect to Your Health Goals at School

Consider ways to meet your health goals while at school. Here are some ideas to get you started:

- **Pack healthy food.** Commit to sticking to the food you come to school with and avoiding the day-old doughnuts and other treats that often fill the staff lounge.
- **Set a hydration goal.** The last thing you need is a headache, so set a goal of finishing your water bottle by lunchtime and refilling it at the end of the day. Let students know about this goal and encourage them to keep you sipping.
- **Move with students.** Whether you are participating in movement breaks with students or joining in on extracurricular activities, make sure you move each day! Not only does this get your body moving and help reset your mind, but it can also increase student engagement and strengthen your relationships with students.

- **Move with staff.** Find a partner to go for a walk with at lunch or after school. This is a great way to not only get exercise but also build relationships.
- **Get outside.** Look for opportunities throughout the day to go outside and get some fresh air. This is a great way to restore energy and reset for the rest of the day.

Promote Mutual Care

If it's important for us as teachers to be healthy and happy at school, it's important for students, too. Practice self-care alongside your students and help them understand how it can increase their happiness and well-being. Not only will they be receiving the care they need, but they will also be better able to focus when it's time for learning. Whenever you can, promote the following self-care essentials:

- **Mindfulness.** Learn about the benefits of mindfulness together with your students and schedule times throughout the day to slow down, get quiet, and be present.
- **Movement.** Physical wellness is directly correlated with emotional wellness. Break up lessons and stretches of learning with structured movement breaks.
- **Healthy eating.** Modeling healthy eating for your students is a great way to promote proper nutrition.
- **Gratitude.** According to Brené Brown (2022), every person she has interviewed "actively practiced gratitude." Gratitude is often said to be the "gateway to happiness." Learn about the importance of practicing gratitude together with students and incorporate gratitude practice in your class meetings or community circles. Train your brains together to see more positives than negatives.
- **Kindness.** The fastest way to increase your own happiness is to be others-oriented and lift others up. Spend time learning about the impact of intentional acts of kindness with your class and find creative ways to promote kindness throughout the classroom and school. Be sure to point out how acts of kindness toward others benefit everyone involved.

LESSONS LEARNED

At my previous school, there was a group of women who referred to themselves as the GATs—short for "Girls Around Town." They always sat together at lunch, laughing and planning their next outing together. They seemed to be having so much fun that I eventually took to sitting with them at lunch. I think they enjoyed having a male perspective in the group. They even named me an honorary GAT and made me a T-shirt. Although they never invited me on their shopping trips, it was amazing to spend time each week in their group. The GATs taught me about the importance of finding your people at work, prioritizing them, and just having fun together with colleagues.

—Rob

Establish and Maintain Happy and Healthy Routines at Home

Throughout this book, we've tried to show that happiness and well-being are inside jobs; it's up to *us* to be a part of our own rescue and move toward feeling more grounded, steady, aligned, and balanced. Well-being is not found, it's created, and well-being routines can make a big difference in our overall happiness.

Following are some well-being routines that Suzanne prioritizes in her daily life. Consider this an invitation for you to examine or start some of your own well-being routines.

Suzanne's Morning Routines

My morning routine actually begins the night before. Each night, I make sure two things are ready for the morning: coffee and clothes. Before I go upstairs to bed, I make sure the coffeemaker is set to automatically start brewing at 5:00 a.m. This helps "tomorrow Suzanne" tremendously. Then I walk upstairs, and as I brush my teeth, I grab my workout clothes and put them by the bathroom sink.

Fast-forward to the morning. I wake up about an hour before my husband and kids. My alarm goes off, and there are my workout clothes laid out for me. Since research shows that physical wellness is directly connected to our emotional wellness and cognition (Ratey with Hagerman, 2008), it's something I want to do each day. Having my exercise clothes laid out ahead of time allows me to decrease my "activation energy"—I don't have to go find my workout clothes and risk losing motivation.

I put on my clothes in less than 20 seconds, then go downstairs and start to enjoy the coffee that is there waiting for me. During this time, it's important for me to be alone and in complete stillness. Time spent in stillness is another universal practice of happiness, and this is a realistic time to incorporate it into my day. I sit quietly with my coffee for about 15–20 minutes.

Around 5:30 a.m., I head to the basement and spend 20–30 minutes moving my body. I can't say I always love walking down the stairs to exercise, but I can absolutely say I love how I feel when I walk back up. One hundred percent of the time, when I exercise in the morning, I have more patience, energy, and creativity and feel more productive the rest of the day.

Suzanne's Afternoon Routine

At 3:30 p.m., an alarm goes off on my phone with a reminder that says "text." This allows me to practice yet another universal practice of happiness: strengthening social relationships. I send a quick text or email to check in with someone in my personal or professional life, thank them for something, or just share a quick emoji. Reaching out to someone I care about also incorporates another universal practice of happiness, performing an intentional act of kindness—and if I am thanking them, it can also include gratitude. This 10-second routine adds a significant amount of happiness to my day.

Suzanne's Evening Routines

Around 8:30 p.m., I put away my phone for the night. I stop replying to texts, I stop scrolling, and I try getting into a calm, content space. After brushing my teeth and putting out my workout clothes, it's time for my most impactful daily practice: writing in my gratitude journal, which I've been doing since 1997. I take a few seconds to write down two or three great things that happened that day.

Then I climb into bed and read a book of fiction. Getting lost in someone else's story allows me to tune out of my own for a bit, tires my eyes, and helps me fall asleep. We all know that getting enough sleep is essential to feeling our best. It's another universal practice of happiness.

Quiet time, exercise, stillness, a quick text, gratitude, reading, getting enough sleep—all of these are ways to have a good day on purpose. Routines are not meant to make our lives feel rigid or overly structured, but to help ensure that we will feel good.

So make it a good day. Make it a good night. With purpose. *On* purpose.

Reflect on Your Routines

Teacher and author Dan Tricarico (2021) suggests using the following questions to reflect on our daily routines:

- **What can I subtract?** The answer to this question can help us say no to the right things so we can bring some stillness into our lives.
- **Whom can I help?** Connect with others and strengthen your relationships.
- **Whom or what am I grateful for?** Reflecting on this question is one way to practice gratitude.
- **Where is my silence?** Seek out pockets of stillness as you move through busy days.
- **What is my wellness practice?** This open-ended question invites you to consider what moves the dial in your own life. Maybe it's walking your dog, watching a favorite show, or listening to a favorite podcast. Whatever it is, it contributes to your general well-being.

Choose a Positive Reality

One of our favorite authors is Shawn Achor. His books on happiness have helped to shape our understanding of positive psychology and the power of tapping into more joy in our lives. In his 2010 book *The Happiness Advantage*, Achor makes the point that "our interpretation of reality changes our experience of reality" (p. 7). In other words, we have the power to see reality itself in different ways *if we choose to*. When thinking about a situation, we can *choose* to focus on either *positive reality* or *negative reality*. According to Achor, those who are the happiest and most successful are those who see the different potential realities of the same situation and choose the one that benefits them the most.

During the pandemic, the term *toxic positivity* became a major topic of conversation in education and beyond. Essentially, toxic positivity is "the act of avoiding, suppressing, or rejecting negative emotions or experiences. This may take the form of denying your own emotions or someone else denying your emotions, insisting on positive thinking instead" (*Psychology Today,* n.d., para. 1). To avoid toxic positivity, we want to acknowledge the negative *and* the positive aspects of our experiences.

We recommend following these steps to avoid both negativity and toxic positivity when facing a challenging situation:

1. Start by relaxing and getting yourself in a positive headspace, where you are open to viewing your situation more objectively.
2. Write down what you feel is the current reality of the situation. Be honest about how you're feeling about it.
3. Make a list of all the negative emotions or experiences you are having related to the situation.
4. Make a list of everything that is going well with the situation.
5. Look for positive aspects of the situation that you might have previously been neglecting and consider how they might affect your happiness.

LESSONS LEARNED

During the pandemic, my wife and I bought an aboveground pool. The box said it was easy to put up, so I dragged it into my backyard and began to assemble it.

One of my neighbors said that I needed to put it on sand. I had not thought of that, but it made sense, so I went out and bought a truckful of sand. It took me most of the day to wheelbarrow it all into my backyard, but I did it. Then I opened the box and assembled the pool. Eventually, I had it sitting perfectly on the sand, ready to be filled with water.

Before filling the pool, I decided to look at the instructions, which I hadn't read yet. Very clearly, they said not to place the pool on top of grass or sand. I, of course, had put it on *both* grass and sand. Though I was frustrated, embarrassed, and tired, I grabbed a shovel and started digging out an area elsewhere on the lawn where I could put the pool.

Eventually, my wife came out and told me to throw in the towel for the night. After dinner, I went outside with a drink to look at the mess I'd created in my backyard. It was at that point that I asked myself what the positive reality of this situation was. It did not take long before an answer popped into my head. My wife was confused by how quickly my emotions changed.

So what was the positive reality? Now we had a pool *and* a beach in the backyard!

—Rob

Maximize Your Mentor

Here are some questions to ask your mentor toward the end of the school year:

- What essential end-of-year responsibilities should I prepare for?
- What resources should I revisit to refine my practice for next year?

LESSONS LEARNED

One of my mom's greatest fears was dying alone. The day she was admitted into palliative care, we had a family meeting to discuss taking shifts to look after her around the clock. During that meeting, we decided that my dad would be the first to go home. My sister said to him, "Go home and don't do anything. Just relax."

My dad responded that he was going to cut the grass. My sister encouraged him not to worry about the grass. What he said next helped shape my understanding of self-care: "But Laura, cutting the grass is what makes me feel good."

Later that evening, I had to go and pick something up near his house. As I drove by, I saw his lawnmower sitting on the side of the lawn, but no sign of him. I started to worry—until I saw him on the other side of the street looking over at his grass with a smile. For many people, cutting the grass is a chore, but for my dad it is something that fills his cup and that he takes great pride in.

—Rob

Take Care of School-Year You

We have often used the exercise in Figure 5.2 to help educators figure out a self-care plan. When reviewing one another's plans, they regularly discover things that they hadn't thought of and decide to give them a try. Everyone's ideas of self-care are different:

- Some want to do something that is low-energy and mindless.
- Some want to burn off negative energy to get the stress out.
- Some want to delve into a passion and enter a state of flow.
- Some want to distract themselves from the stresses of the day.
- Some want to be pampered and indulge in luxuries.

Whatever you put in your self-care plan, know that if it works for you, that is all that matters.

FIGURE 5.2 **Self-Care Plan**

Step 1: In the space around the central box below, write as many things as you can that make you feel better for a sustained period.

Step 2: Inside the central box, write "My Self Care Plan."

Don't Overdo It

Make sure you don't take your self-care activities too far and negate their benefits (see Figure 5.3). It's important to find the sweet spot that works best for you.

Use the Wellness Wheel Inventory

Think back to August you—the version of you who made all those wonderfully optimistic (and, possibly, unrealistic) goals for yourself. When the freshness of a new school year fades, it can be difficult to stay focused on what inspired us back before students arrived. To recapture some of that focus, consider using the wellness wheel inventory strategy. There are many versions of the wellness wheel (see Figure 5.4), but the wellness model was originally developed by Bill Hettler (1980), cofounder of the National Wellness Institute.

The modern wellness wheel consists of the following eight dimensions:

- **Physical:** movement, nutrition, rest
- **Emotional:** feelings, coping
- **Intellectual:** learning new things, applying knowledge
- **Spiritual:** connecting to universe
- **Social:** connecting to others, feeling supported
- **Occupational:** job fulfillment

FIGURE 5.3 **Risks Associated with Too Much Self-Care**

Self-Care Activity	Potential Risks
Watching TV	Spending too much time watching TV can make you feel lazy and unmotivated to do other important tasks, leading to more stress in the future.
Working out	Overtraining your body can result in a repetitive-strain injury that negatively affects your ability to get the movement you need.
Writing	Some people get so obsessed with writing or other hobbies that they start ignoring their family and responsibilities. (We speak from experience.)
Scrolling on your phone	Doomscrolling can saturate your mind with so much negativity that it affects your ability to focus, and excessive scrolling on social media can invite unhealthy habits such as impulse shopping and comparing your life with the seemingly ideal ones presented online.
Getting a massage	Splurging on luxuries can add up in the long run and become a stressful financial burden.

- **Financial:** decisions about money
- **Environmental:** our homes, communities, planet

The goal is to figure out which parts of the wellness wheel are present and active in your life, and which parts deserve a bit more focused attention. The way to do this is to color in the wheel according to this scale:

- 10 (exceeding expectations)
- 8–9 (great!)
- 5–7 (satisfactory)
- 1–4 (needs improvement)

Looking at Figure 5.4, think about how you'd rate each dimension in your life. After you've assigned a number to each section, take a moment to reflect on the areas you'd like to see improvement in. Once you've identified your growth areas, consider creating a plan so you can make some small shifts to help you achieve that growth.

FIGURE 5.4 **The Wellness Wheel**

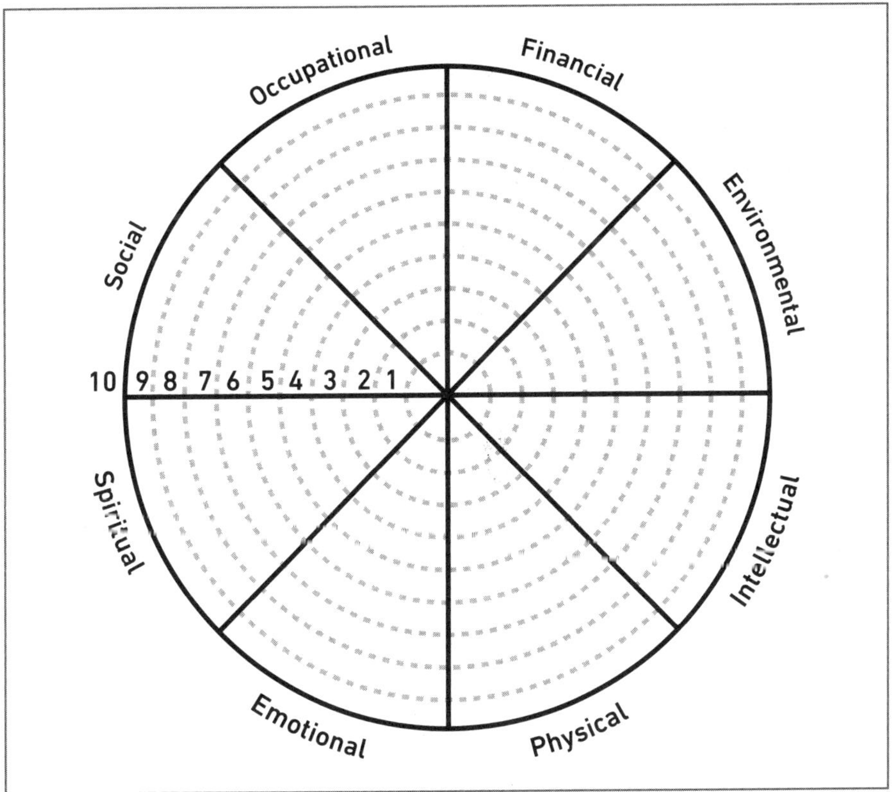

Figure 5.5 shows a wellness wheel completed by Suzanne. The shading indicates that Suzanne is doing well at creating time and space for social connection, physical wellness, and creative work. It also shows areas that could benefit from more attention: It's pretty clear that Suzanne's next right thing is to gain a stronger understanding of financial matters and improve the physical environment of her home, workspace, or community. Completing this exercise helped Suzanne's areas of growth come into focus.

Any social, physical, or emotional goals we make in our personal or professional lives are put in place to strengthen our focus, happiness, and success. But routine school days are filled with lots of routine things, and it's easy to lose sight of the promises we make to ourselves at the beginning of the school year. Slow down just a bit to check in on your wellness so you can keep moving toward contentment, fulfillment, and, ultimately, happiness.

FIGURE 5.5 **Suzanne's Filled-In Wellness Wheel**

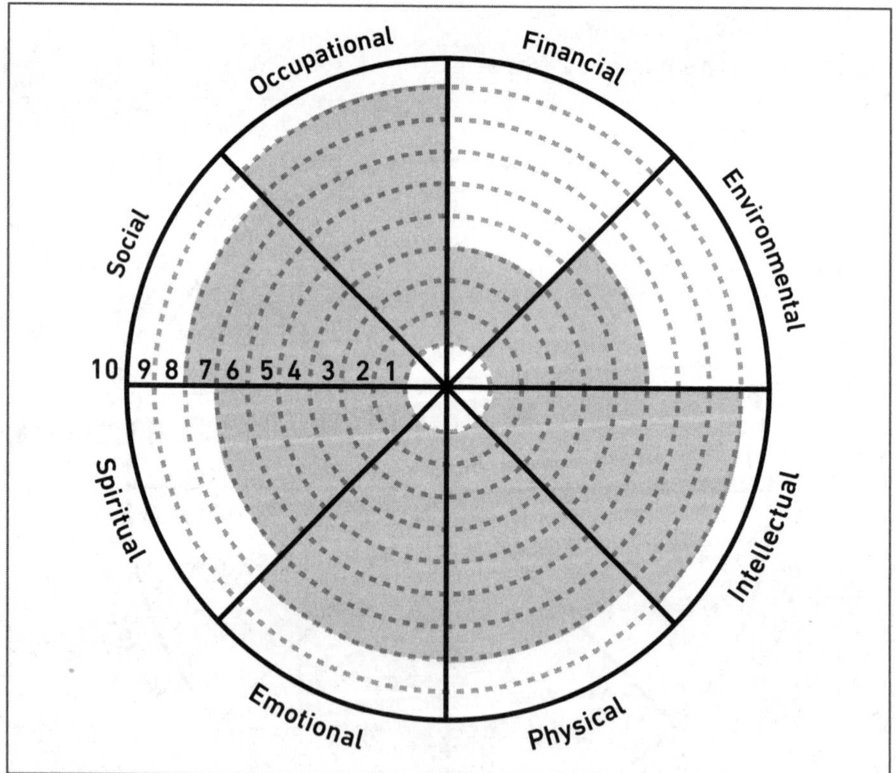

CHAPTER 5 CHECKLIST

We hope this chapter's strategies help you sustain the success you have generated up to this point in the year. Your success and growth can serve as a great base to build on until school is out. Stay positive and continue to look for new ways to hone your teaching style and keep students engaged and learning!

Happiness and Success for Your Students and Classroom

- ☐ Choose an upcoming lesson to record and watch to reflect on your strengths and goal areas.
- ☐ Reach out to a veteran teacher and ask if you can observe them.
- ☐ Consider what practice you want to start, stop, continue, or consider in the future.
- ☐ Take time right now to recognize someone who you believe is doing a great job in your school.
- ☐ Evaluate how much you are investing in finding joy with your students.
- ☐ Conduct an "energy audit" to determine where your limited energy goes.
- ☐ Commit to one or two ways to connect your health goals to your teaching.
- ☐ Answer the five questions recommended by Dan Tricarico on page 124.
- ☐ Tackle tough situations by looking for multiple realities and choosing the one with the most positive outcome.

Happiness and Success for You

- ☐ Find your green-flag colleagues. Try to do one thing to nurture that collegial relationship.
- ☐ Ask yourself reflective questions to honor your accomplishments, boundaries, creativity, and goals.
- ☐ Make a list of two or three home routines that contribute to your well-being.
- ☐ Create a self-care plan that aligns with what actually makes you feel better in the long term.
- ☐ Make a list of your self-care habits and make sure not to overdo them.
- ☐ Complete the wellness wheel inventory and reflect on where you need to direct more attention.

CHAPTER

6

Read in Case of Emergency: Tackling Common First-Year Challenges

You will notice that this chapter is organized differently than the others. As we mentioned in our opening letter at the start of this book, we have collectively worked with thousands of new teachers during the last 15 years and seen just about everyone go through the same challenges. Here, we explore common obstacles and provide strategies for successfully addressing them. You can think of this as a "break in case of emergency" chapter: Turn to it whenever you're facing the following challenges:

- You are nervous about an upcoming observation (see p. 134).
- You had an unsuccessful lesson (see p. 135).
- You need support with student behavior (see p. 137).
- You want to better prioritize tasks (see p. 139).
- You feel disconnected from colleagues (see p. 142).
- You are working with a challenging parent (see p. 143).
- You don't feel you are connecting with your principal (see p. 145).
- You are comparing yourself negatively with others (see p. 147).
- You are struggling to balance work and home (see p. 149).
- You feel overwhelmed and exhausted (see p. 150).

You Are Nervous About an Upcoming Observation

Pre-observation nerves are not only common but also an expected part of the job. If you find yourself worrying about what could go wrong, remember the two main things you can control: how you *prepare* and how you *respond*.

LESSONS LEARNED

I've been teaching for 23 years, and I still get nervous every time I am observed—which, as an instructional coach teaching model lessons, can be multiple times a day! Feeling nervous as colleagues observe my work is inevitable. I try to make a small shift in my mindset and remember that I am nervous because I care. I care deeply about teaching and want it to be a meaningful experience for the students and the teacher (or teachers) observing me. When I recognize that my increased heart rate is due to my dedication, it makes it a bit easier for me to welcome those feelings.

—Suzanne

Prepare

Prior to the observation, think about the things within your realm of control that you can adequately prepare for:

- **Lesson plans.** Take the time to be sure your lesson plans are visible and complete and show evidence of reflection.
- **Lesson materials.** Reread your lesson plans. Do you have all the materials necessary for you and your students?
- **Classroom organization.** How does your classroom look? Is it organized and clear of unnecessary clutter? Remember this quote from Gretchen Rubin (2019): "Outer order contributes to inner calm" (p. 1).
- **Professional attire.** How do you look for your observation? Are you professionally dressed to command the room?

Respond

You may not be able to control what your students say or do during the observation, but you can absolutely control how you respond. Here are some common issues that may crop up and corresponding responses that we've found to be successful:

- **A student raises their hand and says, "I don't get it."** "Thanks for letting me know. Can you please tell me which part is confusing or where in the lesson you started to not understand?"
- **A student is not paying attention.** Move physically closer to the student. When the class is focused on work, check in with the student and ask them what they need to stay focused.
- **Your pacing is off and you are running out of time.** "Since you are doing well with the first and second example, we're going to skip three and four and try number five next."
- **Most students aren't showing progress toward the learning goal.** "I'm noticing most of us are confused. Let's slow down and try a few more examples together."
- **Students are wiggly.** "We are going to take a quick brain break. Everyone stand, and let's do our [insert energizer activity] before we move on."
- **You feel your face getting red due to nerves.** Just. Keep. Going. You can always share in your post-observation conversation that you get nervous when observed. Administrators will understand!

Preparing how to calmly react to unexpected situations can help alleviate some of the natural nerves you feel before an observation. Just remember, this reaction shows how deeply you care about this profession and your students.

You Had an Unsuccessful Lesson

Yep, this is inevitable. You will undoubtedly have a lesson that flops. Even the most meticulously planned lessons can elicit blank stares from a classroom of students. It's OK. Give yourself grace. Then give yourself some time to reflect and think about why the lesson didn't go as planned. Here are some questions to consider:

- Did students have enough prior knowledge to understand the material?
- When in the lesson did you notice the most student engagement? Why do you think that happened during that part of the lesson?

- When in the lesson did you notice a decrease in student engagement? Why do you think that happened during that part of the lesson?
- Was the concept too easy or too difficult for students to learn?
- How was the pacing? Did the lesson move too quickly? Too slowly?
- What teaching strategy did you use (e.g., direct instruction, classroom conversation, cooperative learning)? Would students interact with the content better if you used a different teaching strategy?

When you see your students after reflecting on these questions, let them know you thought the lesson would go differently and explain how you will approach it today (e.g., review key concepts, reteach altogether, try a different approach).

LESSONS LEARNED

A turning point for me this year occurred after I had the most disengaged math class of all time. There was zero interest, motivation, participation, or even signs of life in pretty much every student. Regardless of how easy I made the questions, I still got nothing. I felt that I had planned a good lesson and broken the learning down effectively, but they were not having it.

Instead of getting mad at my students or making them feel bad about it, the next day I asked them what happened and what we could do to make sure it never happened again. They told me that it had a lot to do with the class before mine; their disengagement there had transferred to my class. So we decided to take a little movement break between classes. The students also recommended using individual whiteboards to increase participation, so I got each of them a whiteboard—and wow, what a game changer! It went from several hands up to give answers to pretty much the entire class participating on each question. The whiteboards also gave me a clear understanding of where each student was and when it was time to move on. We continued to use these whiteboards in most lessons for the rest of the year.

What I learned from this was that bad lessons can lead to good learning about my students and myself. Taking the time to discuss together what went wrong is a great strategy to ensure it does not happen as much.

—Rob

You Need Support with Student Behavior

As educators, we want to de-escalate instances of disruptive behavior whenever we can. Here are a few strategies for doing so:

- Stop and address the behavior in the moment to prevent it from getting worse. Later, address the behavior in greater detail in a class meeting to help unpack it and explore solutions as a class.
- Have the student or students role-play different situations to practice a more appropriate response.
- Encourage peer accountability by having students remind one another of classroom expectations.

Remind yourself that students aren't so much *giving* you a hard time as they are *having* a hard time. This will help you depersonalize the situation a bit. It's also a good idea to consider what the underlying function of the behavior could be so you can determine the most appropriate intervention. Figure 6.1 shows the most common functions for different behaviors.

Remember, as teachers, we model not only how to complete academic tasks but also emotional regulation. When you intervene to support your students, it's important to speak in a clear yet respectful tone, use positive language (e.g., "Let's work together on this"), and provide choices whenever possible (e.g., "Would you like to complete your math at the back table or your desk?"). If the interventions you try aren't working, we encourage you to ask your mentor, school counselor, or principal if there are any behavior specialists on staff to help you.

Understand That Students Want Power and Attention

No matter their age, all students are looking for two things: power and attention.

By *power*, we simply mean that students are looking to have some say in what's happening. Could you offer students choice regarding the order in which they complete assignments? Or allow them to give feedback on what's working or not working in the classroom? (This may sound scary at first, but imagine the power they'll feel knowing you're listening to their suggestions about the learning environment!) Perhaps there are classroom

FIGURE 6.1 **Four Functions of Behavior: SEAT**

Function	What It Looks Like	How to Address It
Sensory	Some students want to stimulate sensory pleasure in their brains, especially if they are excited or anxious.	If a student is showing sensory behaviors, providing a fidget, chewing gum, or flexible seating could potentially help.
Escape	Students want to get out of an undesired activity or situation. This may occur when a student is bored, is overstimulated, or simply doesn't want to complete the task in front of them.	A helpful strategy in this case could sound like this: "As soon as you are done with your math sheet, you can play a math game on your iPad." Other strategies would be to offer choice (e.g., "Would you like to complete the reading first or start on your writing?") or simply break up the task into manageable chunks so it seems a bit more reasonable to your student.
Attention	Students are seeking attention in inappropriate, distracting ways.	One proactive strategy to address this need is to introduce appropriate ways to seek attention and then give immediate positive feedback to reinforce expected behavior. It can be difficult to do, but if the attention-seeking behavior isn't disrupting the learning of other students, it's sometimes effective to try and ignore it altogether.
Tangible	A student may want something tangible and may demonstrate behavior to see if they can get it.	One way to support this behavior function is to teach waiting and requesting skills and immediately reinforce them when used. Try your best not to give in to the request, as you don't want to convey that the undesired behavior will allow a student to get something. Instead, consider using a token system or visual schedule to communicate when students would be able to have access to the desired item.

responsibilities you can assign to students so they feel they are making a contribution.

Attention, of course, means students want to be noticed. There are many ways to help them meet this need (e.g., complimenting them on their efforts; checking in on them during a challenging time; celebrating academic, social, or extracurricular accomplishments). Give your students just a little power and attention and see what that can do for your relationships.

One tip: Remember to always be consistent. Students will get frustrated if they notice inconsistencies in how you manage the class. Be as fair as possible, and make sure students can safely predict the consequences of not following the rules.

LESSONS LEARNED

On my return to the classroom, I had quite a challenging class. In the first couple of months, I was taking it very personally. In my mind, I was planning great lessons and doing my best to build relationships and engage my students. So when a student was being disruptive and disrespectful, it really got to me.

It was not until I truly began to learn my students' personal stories that I realized some of their behaviors had less to do with me and more to do with what they were struggling with. As my empathy for them grew, I was better able to understand their outbursts. They were still challenging to deal with at times, but my approach changed greatly. Instead of getting my back up and escalating the issue, I learned how to approach these situations in a softer way and work on *de*-escalating them.

Now when students are disruptive in class, I give them a little time and space to regulate themselves and then engage them in a one-on-one conversation about what occurred in class. I usually start by asking how they are doing and whether everything is all right. Often, they will share something that is happening at home, or that they did not sleep well or are "hangry." These insights give me a better understanding of what students are dealing with and sometimes lead to a simple solution, like providing a snack. By asking how they're doing, I show students that I care about them and that I want them to be successful in my class. This also gives me the platform to share how their actions are affecting me and the rest of the class and reiterate expectations.

—Rob

You Want to Better Prioritize Tasks

In an effort to be productive either at home or at school, we often try to do more than one thing at a time. All of us have heard of multitasking, and some of us would even say we are really good at it. But have you heard of *monotasking*? This is a new term for us, but it's starting to go mainstream: "Monotasking, also known as single-tasking, is the practice of dedicating oneself to a given task and minimizing potential interruptions until the task is completed or a significant period of time has elapsed" (Far, 2017, para. 1).

In 2022, Brené Brown interviewed neuroscientist Amishi Jha on her podcast *Dare to Lead*. In their discussion, Jha used the metaphor of a flashlight to describe monotasking. When you use a flashlight, you can only really focus on whatever it's illuminating; everything else is fuzzed out. Or think of turning down the music in the car when you're trying to follow directions. Sometimes we *have* to monotask.

Multitasking or "task switching" is hard on our brains because it requires us to constantly switch our focus from one thing to another. As Jennifer Davis (2023) notes, "This constant switching taxes our brain. It essentially tires it out and makes it less efficient. This particularly affects our ability to focus our attention in general, even when we are not multitasking" (para. 2). By contrast, monotasking allows us to move through our tasks (chosen or not) and our days feeling a bit more connected and a bit more present.

So, when you find yourself in a frenzied state of multitasking, try to notice when it's hindering your ability to do tasks well and consider monotasking instead. See what you can put down to keep the main thing the main thing. Shine that flashlight on what's important, let the other things fuzz out, and see if this affects your overall feelings of contentment or happiness.

Put a Language to Your Limitations

To quote Prentis Hemphill (2021), "Boundaries are the distance at which I can love you and me simultaneously." In other words, boundaries put language to our limitations. To preserve your limited bandwidth, try not to overstep the boundaries you've set for yourself. How can you love and care for others and yourself simultaneously?

We aren't limitless. We need limitations. Try putting language to your limitations.

LESSONS LEARNED

When someone asks me, "Hey, Suzanne, do you have a minute?" they often mean far more than a minute, and I am grateful for those connecting, productive conversations. But if I have a lot to get done, I can get frustrated knowing that my needs can't be met because I am meeting someone else's. That's when I think back to the Prentis Hemphill quote. So what do I do? I say, "Yes! Let's chat! I'll set a timer for 15 minutes so I can be sure I leave time to get this other task done."

—Suzanne

LESSONS LEARNED

Early in the year, a student emailed me with concerns about some other students. It was not urgent, but I decided to respond. Then the student responded to my response, and eventually my night was consumed with this issue that I could not do anything about.

When I arrived at school the next day, I told my principal about the emails. She was quick to advise me not to respond to messages like the one I had received after school during my time to disconnect and be with family. By immediately responding to emails, she said, I was conditioning students to think that I am always on call. She told me that I needed to set clear boundaries instead, and to keep in mind that some things can seem much more urgent than they actually are. This student's issue could definitely have waited until the morning, as there was nothing I could have done that evening to resolve the situation.

I learned then that for my own well-being, I needed to change my habits around communication. I now realize that not responding immediately does not mean that I do not care about my students, but that I *also* care about myself and my family.

—Rob

You Feel Disconnected from Colleagues

Positive psychologists (Achor, 2010) tell us that 100 percent of happy people have one thing in common: strong social relationships. The easiest way to form such relationships is to find someone who is interested in the same things you are (e.g., the same sports team, the same vacation spot). Common interests give us a natural starting point for future conversations. And how do you find out whether you have interests in common with someone? Ask good questions.

Try to Do Something Outside School

Some days, it is tough to muster up the energy to be socially active, but proactively spending time with colleagues outside work can help you thrive *at* work. Conversations around a restaurant table feel different than they do in a faculty room or staff lounge and can help you forge a deeper bond with others.

Find Your Teacher Friends Forever (TFFs)

As you move throughout your career, you will meet other educators you connect with on many levels. Make a point of extending yourself to these people. They will be the ones who will be there throughout the good and the bad. Even as you change schools or roles, continue to reach out and find ways to connect. These relationships are worth the investment.

As a new teacher, you may find that forging new connections takes a little time, but do not give up. Keep persevering. Eventually, you will find your people.

LESSONS LEARNED

The first couple of months into my return to the classroom, I felt overwhelmed and like I had little time or energy to do things for myself. I was fixated on doing a great job in the classroom, so I was using my lunches and prep periods to get work done. I tended to keep to myself unless someone approached me, and I kept a very tight circle.

At one point, I was approached about joining several other teachers to play basketball against some students. At first, I declined the invitation, as I felt I did not have the energy or time. However, after popping my head into the gym after school one day and seeing how much fun they were having, I decided to give it a shot.

Despite feeling rusty and out of shape, this hour of basketball became one of the things I looked forward to the most each week. Being new to the school, I loved getting to know students on a different level and in different ways. It did not take long before they were trash-talking me in the hallways and asking if I was playing that week.

One of the best things to develop from Friday-night basketball was the camaraderie with other staff members. Very quickly, work relationships developed into friendships. We became a team on and off the court, which really helped make me feel more connected to colleagues. These relationships are now among my favorite parts of my job. On top of all that, I've gotten in better shape and feel more energetic. Looking back, I realize that I needed to put myself out there if I was going to make meaningful connections with both staff and students.

—Rob

You Are Working with a Challenging Parent

New teachers, master teachers, and all teachers in between will encounter parents who question their decisions, demand explanations, or find creative ways to gauge their skill sets as educators. It can be nerve-racking at times, but it's also completely normal, especially in your first year.

If a parent is challenging you now, it's likely they've challenged one of your colleagues before. To gain some perspective, it is wise to ask one of the student's former teachers about the parent—preferably in person rather than in writing, as it's easier to misconstrue the tone of written messages. In addition, keep in mind that anything you say in an email or other written message could be disclosed via "right to know" laws, which grant parents access to their child's education records. So don't write anything that you wouldn't want others to read! You can start with something like this: "You had Ryan

Dailey last year, right? His parents are upset about [insert issue]. Was this your experience with them? If so, can you help me think through ways to appropriately approach them so we can come to some kind of solution?"

Call, Don't Write

It's often better to call upset parents than to get into a back-and-forth email exchange, as this enables both of you to better understand the other's intended tone, which can be hard to read in writing. Hearing one another's voices adds a bit of humanity to a challenging situation. If you have a mentor or other trusted colleague, consider putting the call on speakerphone so they can help you navigate the conversation.

Follow Up with Something Positive

After talking through an issue with a parent, set a calendar reminder to follow up with positive news and do what you can to proactively repair the relationship. Always remember that when parents are being challenging, it is usually their way of showing that they care and trying to support their child. Taking the time to understand this will help you build better relationships with students' families.

LESSONS LEARNED

In my first year of teaching, I had a parent challenge me on a test score. I was nervous about explaining why I had marked an answer as wrong, especially since I was new to the district. My mentor suggested that I discuss the situation with the parent over the phone rather than by email. Together, we rehearsed what I was going to say, and I took notes so I could be prepared. When I spoke to the parent, I did so on speakerphone, with my mentor sitting nearby to encourage me, suggest language to use (hastily written on a dry-erase board), and generally help me navigate the conversation. Being able to hear each other's voices helped the parent and me interpret the tone of the conversation more accurately and reach a resolution. Afterward, I realized that calling a parent can actually *save* time. Engaging in an ongoing email exchange about the issue would have ultimately taken much more time than

our five-minute phone call did. In addition, I knew this parent appreciated the time I took to call. In the end, I felt confident that taking a few minutes to call home can strengthen the home-school relationship.

—Suzanne

You Don't Feel You Are Connecting with Your Principal

As a new teacher, building deep relationships with other teachers can be easier than building a strong relationship with your principal. There are natural opportunities to connect with other teachers such as lesson planning, extracurriculars, and time spent in the staff room. Due to the nature of their jobs, however, administrators are pulled in many directions, making it hard for them to spend quality time with teachers.

The first thing to remember is not to take this personally. Administrators would love to spend more time getting to know you, but they are usually putting out unexpected fires all day. It's not that they don't *want* to spend time with you, it's that they don't *have* the time. You can feel confident that if you are doing the following things, they are probably happy with you:

- Arriving to school on time
- Completing supervision duties
- Trying to handle classroom issues yourself before sending students to the office
- Showing interest and engagement during staff meetings
- Being kind to staff and students
- Being a positive influence in school

When you are looking to have a quality conversation with your principal, timing is everything. There are definitely times in a principal's day that are busier than others. To show that you honor your principal's time, you can email them and say something like, "Hi, Dr. Dunlop, I'd like to talk to you about [insert student/topic]. What time would work best for us to chat this through?" See Figure 6.2 for some suggestions for when and when not to approach administrators.

FIGURE 6.2 **Best and Worst Times to Connect with Administrators**

Best Times to Connect	Why?
Right after morning announcements	Students are most regulated at the start of the day, so behavioral issues are less likely to arise at this time. Your principal should have a pocket of availability.
About 20 minutes after school is dismissed	The end of the day can be chaotic, and often many staff are looking to connect with administration before they go home. Do a little planning of your own first, giving the principal time before you approach them after school.
Professional development days	This is your best time to connect with your principal. You are their focus on this day, and there are few distractions, so make a point of going out of your way to have a conversation with them.
Worst Times to Connect	**Why?**
Right before the school day starts	During this time, administrators are usually preparing to make announcements, dealing with substitute teaching coverages, and putting out fires. Unless it really can't wait, try to give them space right before the day starts.
Right after less structured times of day (e.g., lunch, recess, study hall)	One of the busiest times for principals is during and after less structured times of the school day, when they are often dealing with issues that have cropped up.
Immediately after school	The end of the day can be hectic for principals, who might need to connect with students or parents before they leave work.

Highlight the Good

To build and maintain a positive connection with your principal, try to highlight the good that is happening with your students. When you see the principal in passing, quickly update them on a breakthrough you made with a student or something great that occurred in your class. Principals love to hear about student success stories in the building, so don't be hesitant to share them.

LESSONS LEARNED

Before I returned to the classroom in 2024, I was lucky enough to be a vice principal of a relatively large and complex school—a role that was truly eye-opening for me. Before I started the job, I made myself a vision board of

what I believe a great leader does, with the intention of reflecting on it at the start of every day. I don't think I had the opportunity to look it over once!

One of the points I highlighted on my vision board was to connect with each educator before the day started. Despite knowing how important this is, I rarely had the time to do it. I did not anticipate the number of issues that would present themselves prior to the students even arriving. I had a revolving door of educators asking questions and sharing information.

What I appreciated the most during those busy moments was when a teacher would say to me, "You look busy, can you connect with me later in the day when you have a moment?" I really liked this because if I *had* tried to connect with them at that moment, I would not have been able to give my full attention and support.

One of the best relationships I developed in the job was with a teacher who would drop in at the end of the day if I did not look busy. We would just relax and spend time talking about life and school or sharing funny stories of things that happened throughout the day. This teacher had a great sense of when it was a good time to connect, and I really looked forward to those moments. As a veteran teacher, he was aware of what was urgent and what could wait. As a new vice principal, I really appreciated this understanding and believe that it helped us connect on multiple levels.

—Rob

You Are Comparing Yourself Negatively with Others

This advice is going to make you roll your eyes because it's what we tell our students, but here goes:

Keep your eyes on your own paper!

There will be days when you're walking up and down the hallway or maybe scrolling through social media and you notice colleagues doing amazing things: leading students through an incredibly engaging lesson, for example, or theme-ing out their classroom decorations with the flair of an interior decorator. The amazing things others are doing can make you feel a bit inadequate, and that's why you've got to remember to keep your eyes on your own paper. A brilliant quote often attributed to motivational writer and speaker Jon Acuff puts it this way: "Don't compare your beginning to someone else's middle, or your middle to someone else's end." Your beginning is more than good enough—it's downright incredible. But sometimes you have to consciously shift your thinking to believe it.

Positive psychologists claim that social comparison is normal behavior and can be useful in helping us determine if we're on track. However, psychologist Alicia Nortje (2020) states that comparing ourselves with others against an unrealistic benchmark can be "extremely harmful and result in negative thoughts and behaviors" (para. 2). Instead, take pride in what you've accomplished:

- Are you great with technology and rocking interactive lessons with all the bells and whistles? *Awesome!*
- Are your students growing as readers and writers with simple books and journals? *Phenomenal!*
- Do you have a personalized greeting for each one of your students? *Amazing!*
- Are you quietly checking in on a few students who need to know they are loved? *Spectacular!*
- Do you email a different student's parents every day to compliment their child? *Outstanding!*

At the beginning of our teaching career, we can't always keep pace with everybody else, and that's OK. We are all doing the very best we can for the students in front of us. But if we constantly compare ourselves with others, we will never believe that our best is good enough—and that holds true in the beginning, middle, and end of our careers.

LESSONS LEARNED

One of the most overwhelming things about going back to the classroom after 11 years was the feeling that I was "behind" all my colleagues. Because my previous role in the district was focused on technology, I rarely engaged in professional development on any other subjects, whereas my new colleagues had been learning and honing their skills in all areas for many years.

It was hard for me not to compare what I was doing with what they were doing. They seemed so much more confident and settled than I was. They had also established strong relationships with many of the students in the school, which I had not yet done. I found myself constantly going to them for approval and advice.

I had thought that because I'd left the classroom on a successful note 11 years prior, I would be able to pick up where I left off. This was not the case. I was no longer the leader; I was the new kid. I had to accept that I was starting over again and that it was OK to not have the answers yet. I had to give myself grace and time to learn again.

Eventually, I decided that it was better to focus on my own personal growth than compare myself with others. Once I made that decision, I found that not only was I happier and less stressed out, but I also became more confident about using the skills I had developed in my previous tech-focused role.

At this point in the year, I feel much more confident in so many ways than when I started the year. I am embracing new learning and the journey of being back in the classroom after so much time.

—Rob

You Are Struggling to Balance Work and Home

After an exhausting day at school, have you ever found yourself searching online for something like "strategies to help balance work and home"? If so, you probably came across a bunch of nonscientific articles or Pinterest-perfect quotes that left you feeling less than satisfied. There's a good reason for that: There is actually no such thing as work-life balance.

That's right: Work-life balance simply doesn't exist, which is why it's virtually impossible to attain. Thinking of your own professional and personal life, can you honestly think of a time when you were killing it both at work and at home, giving exactly 50 percent to each place? Of course not! In August, when we're gearing up for the beginning of the school year, we're probably 75 percent "work" and 25 percent "home." The week before winter break, when we are eagerly anticipating celebrations and gatherings with family and friends? We're lucky if we're 20 percent work and 80 percent home. Parent-teacher conference week? Back up to 75 percent at work. If there is a family emergency or a great need at home, we may be 85 percent there and trying to muster up the other 15 percent for work.

This doesn't mean we are doing anything wrong; in fact, it may be the way to do it exactly right. The energy we give to work and home depends on the season and whatever it is we're dealing with at a given time. Part of the reason it's so frustrating when we feel an imbalance is that we've swallowed the narrative that some kind of balance is attainable.

What would happen if we moved away from work-life *balance* and toward work-life *satisfaction* instead?

Can you be balanced in two places simultaneously? Nope.

Can you be *satisfied* in both places simultaneously? Yep. This is attainable.

In your first year of teaching, you will never feel balanced, but you can move the dial a bit by giving yourself some time and space to do what you need to do at home and at school. When you find yourself feeling discouraged by the imbalance, lean into doing something that will help you feel satisfaction.

You Feel Overwhelmed and Exhausted

Are you feeling run down? As we finish one day and race to the next, many of us neglect to give ourselves permission to rest (like, *really* rest). Wouldn't it be great if we could just hit pause and close our eyes to recenter, rejuvenate, and restore?

We can hear you saying, "Rest sounds like a lovely idea, but I can't just shut it down. Not now. *There is so much to do!*"

Yes, there is. But as Kelly Corrigan observes, "Rest is not the opposite of productivity. Rest is productivity's silent partner" (2024).

Read that again: *Rest is productivity's silent partner.*

It can sometimes feel like everything is high-stakes. Leaning into our work with everything we've got can be physically exhausting, cognitively tiresome, and emotionally expensive. Instead, try to manufacture or choreograph pockets of peace and rest—not just to get through the day, but also to *really see* the beauty and magic of what's happening in your life at school and at home.

Want to be productive? Get some rest.

LESSONS LEARNED

As I've already mentioned, the beginning of my first year back was overwhelming for me. I felt that there were a million things I should be doing at all times. For the first couple of months, I worked tirelessly to keep up. My wife kept warning me that I was working too much and that I was going to burn out, and she was right. The more I pushed myself, the less productive I was. Not only that, but I was also starting to feel resentful and frustrated.

So I decided that I needed to make some changes. The first change was to give myself time at the end of the day to decompress. I made sure to carve out 30–45 minutes of time alone at home before my wife and kids showed up. Most days, I would lie down with my dog on the couch and just relax. I began to really enjoy this quiet time and felt that it was positively affecting my mood, giving me the energy I needed to make good use of the rest of my night.

Another issue I was having was trouble getting to sleep. To address this, I decided to disconnect from work about 30 minutes before bedtime. In this time, I would do something I enjoyed, such as watching sports or working on this book. I noticed that when I disconnected from work before bed, I fell asleep more quickly. The sleep-tracking app I use showed improvements in my sleep patterns. I tried my best to ensure that I was getting at least eight hours of sleep each night, having learned that I need this much sleep to feel energized and productive.

Over time, I began to realize that when I took the time to rest, I was more productive and able to do everything I needed to in much less time. I was less stressed and more confident in my ability to use my time effectively. We are not the best versions of ourselves when we are not well rested—so take that well-deserved nap!

—Rob

LESSONS LEARNED

Sometimes it's not realistic for me to not do any schoolwork when I get home, so I try to honor my work and myself by setting boundaries. I turn the ringer off my phone and set a timer for 15–30 minutes and think, "This will be a work sprint. I'll get as much done as I can during this time, and as soon as the timer goes off, I am done working at home."

Getting a few things done at home is important to my wellness—I am less anxious when I don't have a lot of tasks looming the next day—so this is a realistic practice that helps me honor both my personal and my professional life.

—Suzanne

Take Care of School-Year You

In his 2022 book *You, Happier: The 7 Neuroscience Secrets of Feeling Good Based on Your Brain Type,* Daniel Amen discusses decisions we can make to ensure our happiness and health. "You don't have to win the genetic lottery to be blessed with a happy disposition," he writes. "You can learn how to consistently generate positive feelings no matter your age, income, or situation" (p. 3). We couldn't agree more. According to Amen, we should live each day according to our clearly defined values, purpose, and goals. When our actions match our values, we are doing what is within our influence to become a bit happier and healthier.

Amen invites us to examine the four "Circles of Happiness" in our lives: biological, psychological, social, and spiritual. Within each circle, he writes, are opportunities for micro-moments of happiness: "When our brain pays attention to micro-moments of happiness, they add up to more overall contentment and satisfaction. . . . The more micro-moments you cherish, the greater your sense of joy" (p. 20). Take this opportunity to reflect on how you are doing in each of the four circles:

- **Biological.** We feel biological happiness after a great night's sleep, after a workout, or when we feel mentally sharp or engaged. We may also feel it when the weather suits us or when we eat or drink something delicious.

- **Psychological.** To promote psychological happiness, try to start your day with a healthy mental routine or by deciding how you want to feel when you go to bed at night. When something challenging happens during the day, do what you can to correct negative thought patterns.
- **Social.** We feel social happiness when we feel connected to family, friends, and colleagues. We leave conversations feeling fulfilled. Another example of social happiness according to Dr. Amen (2022)? Teaching! (Really, it's on page 21 of his book!)
- **Spiritual.** How connected do you feel toward something bigger than yourself? How do you see your role on this planet, and what can you do to fulfill it? Do you feel purposeful and believe you are making a difference in the life of others?

"Focusing on what you love to do is a surefire way to make you happier," Amen writes (2022, p. 23). So pause and reflect: What brings you joy? What do you value? How are you prioritizing your limited time? Performing an informal "happiness audit" can help you discern your next right thing. Do whatever you can to feel a bit more content, aligned, balanced, anchored, steady—or, as the rest of the world calls it, happy.

A Closing Letter from Suzanne and Rob

Dear Reader,

If you are reading this at the end of your first year of teaching, the following adage might ring true: "The days are long, but the years are short." We are sure you've had a mix of fast days, slow days, great days, and challenging days, and before you knew it, the school year had zoomed by.

You'll look back at your first year and you won't believe how much you accomplished while also learning so much about teaching, students, and, most importantly, yourself.

Although this book is meant to support you in your first few years of teaching, we hope it continues to serve you in the next chapter of your career, too. We encourage you to flip back and reflect on the checklists and self-care recommendations to foster happiness and success in the years ahead.

There's a saying that goes, "One day you will tell your story of how you overcame what you went through, and it will become someone else's survival guide." As soon as your next school year, you are going to be seen by new teachers as someone who can offer advice, perspective, and resources.

Hopefully, reading this book has made you feel more optimistic about your future in education. This is an incredibly rewarding career that has the potential to be life-changing for both you and your students. It will be challenging at times, but those challenges will truly prepare you to make a positive difference in the world.

Always remember to give yourself grace. The great thing about education is that we are all learning together. Do not be too hard on yourself; instead, invest that energy into building relationships and developing a positive mindset. If you can do this, you are destined to be an amazing educator.

Thank you for answering the call to teach. Here's to your first years being filled with happiness and success for both you and your students. You've got this!

All the best,
Suzanne and Rob

Acknowledgments

From Suzanne

Pat, Emerson, and Ryan, thank you for knowing how much joy teaching and writing bring to me. You continue to love me in a way that makes me feel held and free, and I will never get over the fact that we get to do life together. I am so proud of our little team and the beautiful life we've co-created.

Olney and Dailey families, your steadfast love and support have always helped inspire me to do the next ambitious thing, which includes this book. I love you and am profoundly grateful for you. GO BILLS!

To my cherished net of close friends from Doylestown to Brockport to Charlotte: Thank you for endlessly cheering me on and celebrating this unique part of my life. You see me, accept me, and love me for exactly who I am, and I am honored you have chosen me to be a part of your heart. Thank you for the countless ways you show up for my little family.

To my balcony of angels cheering me on from up above, especially my beloved Mom, my favorite teacher: You are all with me every day, and I see the good work you are all doing up there. I promise to keep bringing you back into the room and continue your legacy by sharing your stories and lessons to inspire educators all over the world.

To the hundreds of new teachers I've had the privilege to work alongside in my home school district: Thank you for trusting me to be a part of your professional journey. I am so proud of the work we accomplish together, and I am honored to be a part of your classroom family.

Rob, thanks for being my very first co-author. I've learned so much through this process, and I am grateful for your creativity, sense of humor, and genuine kindness. It's wild how the universe makes sure people who should connect with one another, do. I am so proud of us!

From Robert

Melissa, thank you for putting up with all my crazy ideas throughout the years and giving me the most amazing children. Reid and Lauren, watching you grow into incredible humans is my greatest joy, and it fills me with pride. I hope you find careers that bring you as much happiness and fulfillment as teaching has brought me.

To my amazing sister, Laura: I cannot express in words how much teaching together this year has meant to me. With your words of encouragement, amazing advice, and consistent support with planning, you carried me on your back and helped me be successful in my return to the classroom. The endless depth of your kindness and love for your students will forever inspire me.

To my parents, who have always made me feel loved and supported: Dad, I love that you are just as much my friend as you are my father. Thanks for always being there. Mom, I hope you are in the balcony of angels with Suzanne's mom, cheering us on together. I miss you beyond words and love you so much.

Good luck to my niece Emma and nephew Andrew, who are well on their way to becoming teachers. You are about to embark on one of the most fulfilling careers imaginable. Hang on tight, love students, and enjoy every minute of it.

To my amazing group of friends, who surround me with love and support me every day: I am beyond lucky to have you in my life, and I appreciate you. A special shout-out to my TFFs (Teacher Friends Forever)—you know who you are and how much you mean to me.

Kelly and Dorothy, my time spent with you supporting new teachers was pivotal to my writing this book. I appreciate your guidance, expertise, and friendship during our time together.

And to Suzanne—what a ride! From connecting through social media to becoming close friends and now co-authors, this journey has been unforgettable. You are a dream to work with, and I appreciate the compassion and understanding you showed when I was struggling the most. There is no one I would rather have written this book with.

From Both of Us

Susan and Miriam, thank you for giving us a space to connect with new teachers outside our schools. Your patience and creativity have made this project something we are really proud of.

To *all* new teachers: We dedicated this book to you because we deeply believe in this important work and know firsthand how teaching can positively impact the world. Schools need you, students need you, and humanity needs you. Thank you for choosing this profession and being hope in action.

Bibliography

Achor, S. (2010). *The happiness advantage: The seven principles of positive psychology that fuel success and performance at work*. Crown Business.

Achor, S. (2013). *Before happiness: The 5 hidden keys to achieving success, spreading happiness, and sustaining positive change*. Crown Business.

Achor, S. (2018). *Big potential: How transforming the pursuit of success raises our achievement, happiness, and well-being*. Currency.

Agarwal, P. K., & Bain, P. M. (2019). *Powerful teaching: Unleash the science of learning*. Jossey-Bass.

Alexander, R., Aragón, O. R., Bookwala, J., Cherbuin, N., Gatt, J. M., Kahrilas, I. J., Kästner, N., Lawrence, A., Lowe, L., Morrison, R. G., Mueller, S. C., Nusslock, R., Papadelis, C., Polnaszek, K. L., Richter, S. H., Silton, R. L., & Styliadis, C. (2021, February). The neuroscience of positive emotions and affect: Implications for cultivating happiness and wellbeing. *Neuroscience and Biobehavioral Reviews, 121*, 220–249.

Alimujiang, A., Wiensch, A., Boss, J., Fleischer, N. L., Mondul, A. M., McLean, K., Mukherjee, B., & Pearce, C. L. (2019). Association between life purpose and mortality among US adults older than 50 years. *JAMA Network Open, 2*(5). https://doi.org/10.1001/jamanetworkopen.2019.4270

Amen, D. G. (2022). *You, happier: The 7 neuroscience secrets of feeling good based on your brain type*. Tyndale Refresh.

Archer, A. L. (2015, January 8). *Anita Archer elementary series: Instruction must be interactive* [Video]. Ancora Publishing. https://www.youtube.com/watch?v=UWtoZNRstSE

Archer, A. L. (2023, October 4). *Getting them all engaged: The power of active participation* [Conference breakout session]. The Reading League 7th Annual Conference, Syracuse, NY.

Archer, A. L., & Hughes, C. A. (2011). *Explicit instruction: Effective and efficient teaching*. Guilford Press.

Brady, A. (2024, June 30). #304 End of the 2023–2024 school year reflection [Blog post]. *Anita Brady*. https://anitajbrady.wixsite.com/educator/single-post/304-end-of-the-2023-2024-school-year-reflection

Brittle, Z. (2024, September 19). Turn towards instead of away [Blog post]. Gottman. https://www.gottman.com/blog/turn-toward-instead-of-away/

Brown, B. (Host). (2021, February 24). Dr. Edith Eger on recognizing the choices and gifts in our lives [Audio podcast episode]. *Unlocking Us with Brené Brown*. Parcast at Spotify Studios. https://brenebrown.com/podcast/brene-with-dr-edith-eger-on-recognizing-the-choices-and-gifts-in-our-lives/

Brown, B. (Host). (2022, March 21). Dr. Amisha Jha on finding focus and owning your attention [Audio podcast episode]. *Dare to Lead.* Parcast at Spotify Studios and Weird Lucy Productions. https://brenebrown.com/podcast/finding-focus-and-owning-your-attention/

Buettner, D. (2017). *The Blue Zones of happiness: Lessons from the world's happiest people.* National Geographic.

Burns, M. (2024). *EdTech essentials: 12 strategies for every classroom in the age of AI* (2nd ed.). ASCD.

Corrigan, K. (Host). (2024, November 26). Going deep with Dan Harris on recuperation [Audio podcast episode]. *Kelly Corrigan Wonders.* Cadence13. https://podcasts.apple.com/us/podcast/going-deep-with-dan-harris-on-recuperation/id1532951390?i=1000678248071

Cuticelli, M., Collier-Meek, M. A., & Coyne, M. D. (2016). Increasing the quality of Tier 1 reading instruction: Using performance feedback to increase opportunities to respond during implementation of a core reading program. *Psychology in the Schools, 53*(1), 89–105. https://doi.org/10.1002/pits.21884

Dailey, S. (2023). *Teach happier this school year: 40 weeks of inspiration and reflection.* ASCD.

Davis, J. E. (2023, January 26). Multitasking and how it affects your brain health. *Be Well.* Brown University Health. https://www.brownhealth.org/be-well/multitasking-and-how-it-affects-your-brain-health

Dunlop, R. (2020). *STRIVE for happiness in education.* EduMatch.

Ebbinghaus, H. (1885/1913). *Memory: A contribution to experimental psychology.* Teachers College, Columbia University.

Eger, E. E. (2018). *The choice: Embrace the possible.* Scribner.

Eisenbraun, K. (2021, January 28). *The power 9: Healthy habits from Blue Zone inhabitants.* WellRx. https://www.wellrx.com/news/the-power-9-healthy-habits-from-blue-zone-inhabitants/

Far, S. (2017, May 1). Monotasking keeps the brain healthy and you more productive [Blog post]. *Inc.* https://www.inc.com/samira-far/5-monotasking-tips-that-will-save-your-brain-and-make-you-more-successful.html

FISH! Blog. (2023, July 5). 4 steps to choose your attitude—the FISH! Philosophy way [Blog post]. https://fishphilosophy.com/blog/4-steps-choose-your-attitude-fish-philosophy

Fisher, D., & Frey, N. (2019, February). Show & tell: A video column/The micro-teaching advantage. *Educational Leadership, 76*(5), 82–83. https://www.ascd.org/el/articles/the-micro-teaching-advantage

Fisher, D., & Frey, N. (2022, April 1). Getting GREAT at feedback. *Educational Leadership, 79*(7), 22–28. https://www.ascd.org/el/articles/getting-great-at-feedback

García, H., & Miralles, F. (2017). *Ikigai: The Japanese secret to a long and happy life* (H. Cleary, Trans.). Penguin.

Godwin, K. E., Leroux, A. J., Seltman, H., Scupelli, P., & Fisher, A. V. (2022). Effect of repeated exposure to the visual environment on young children's attention. *Cognitive Science, 46*(2), e13093.

Gonzalez, J. (2013, August 9). Find your marigold: The one essential rule for new teachers. *Cult of Pedagogy.* https://www.cultofpedagogy.com/marigolds

Gottman, J. M., & Levenson, R. W. (1992). Marital processes predictive of later dissolution: Behavior, physiology, and health. *Journal of Personality and Social Psychology, 63*(2), 221–233. https://doi.org/10.1037/0022-3514.63.2.221

Harris, D. (2014). *10% happier: How I tamed the voice in my head, reduced stress without losing my edge, and found self-help that actually works—A true story.* Dey Street.

Hattie, J. (2012). *Visible Learning for teachers: Maximizing impact on learning.* Routledge.

Hemphill, P. [@prentishemphill]. (2021, April 5). *Boundaries are the distance at which I can love you and me simultaneously.* Instagram. https://www.instagram.com/p/CNSzFO1A21C

Hettler, B. (1980, May). Wellness promotion on a university campus. *Family and Community Health, 3*(1), 77–95. https://journals.lww.com/familyandcommunityhealth/citation/1980/05000/wellness_promotion_on_a_university_campus.8.aspx

Hurst, S. (Host). (2022, September 27). Words of wisdom: A special *Literacy Talks* episode with Dr. Anita Archer [Audio podcast episode]. *Literacy Talks*. Reading Horizons. https://readinghorizons.com/literacytalks/words-of-wisdom-a-special-literacy-talks-episode-with-dr-anita-archer/

Jackson, R. R. (2011). *How to motivate reluctant learners*. ASCD.

Jackson, R. R. (2013). *Never underestimate your teachers: Instructional leadership for excellence in every classroom*. ASCD.

Jackson, R. R. (2016, February). *Instructional leadership strategies for educators* [Workshop]. Bucks County Intermediate Unit, Doylestown, PA.

Jacobsen, J. (2023, August 7). *An introduction to AI in education*. Britannica Education. https://britannicaeducation.com/blog/ai-in-education/

Jha, A. P. (2022). *Peak mind: Find your focus, own your attention, invest 12 minutes a day*. HarperOne.

Johnson, J. (2020, July 7). What is "decision fatigue"? *Medical News Today*. https://www.medicalnewstoday.com/articles/decision-fatigue

Kabat-Zinn, J. (1994). *Wherever you go, there you are: Mindfulness meditation in everyday life*. Hyperion.

Kaufman, L. M. (2025, February 17). 4 ideas to keep students engaged and thinking in an AI-driven world [Blog post]. *Empower. Collaborate. Connect.* https://laurenmkaufman.com/2025/02/17/4-ideas-to-keep-students-engaged-and-thinking-in-an-ai-driven-world

Kennedy, B. (2022). *Good inside: A guide to becoming the parent you want to be*. Harper Wave.

Kern, L., & Clemens, N. H. (2007). Antecedent strategies to promote appropriate classroom behavior. *Psychology in the Schools, 44*(1), 65–75. https://doi.org/10.1002/pits.20206

Lindemann-Matthies, P., Benkowitz, D., & Hellinger, F. (2021). Associations between the naturalness of window and interior classroom views, subjective well-being of primary school children, and their performance in an attention and concentration test. *Landscape and Urban Planning, 214*, 104146. https://doi.org/10.1016/j.landurbplan.2021.104146

MacSuga-Gage, A. S., & Gage, N. A. (2015). Student-level effects of increased teacher-directed opportunities to respond. *Journal of Behavioral Education, 24*(3), 273–288. https://doi.org/10.1007/s10864-015-9223-2

Miller, J. (2022, March 9). Using the question matrix to teach critical thinking [Blog post]. *The National Network of State Teachers of the Year (NNSTOY)*. https://www.nnstoy.org/stoyblog/using-the-question-matrix-to-teach-critical-thinking

Mooiman, L. (2023, October 13). *Greeting students at the door—Is it worth the extra time?* Laura Mooiman. https://www.lauramooiman.com/post/greeting-students-at-the-door-is-it-worth-the-extra-time

Nortje, A. (2020, April 29). *Social comparison theory & 12 real-life examples*. PositivePsychology.com. https://positivepsychology.com/social-comparison/

OWN. (2011). *Does your face light up? Oprah's lifeclass*. Oprah Winfrey Network. https://www.youtube.com/watch?v=9Jw0Fu8nhOc

Pennsylvania Training and Technical Assistance Network. (n.d.). *Learning environment & engagement*. https://www.pattan.net/Evidence-Based-Practices/Learning-Environment-Engagement

Porosoff, L. (2023). *Teach for authentic engagement*. ASCD.

Psychology Today. (n.d.). Toxic positivity. https://www.psychologytoday.com/ca/basics/toxic-positivity

Puentedura, R. R. (2013). *SAMR: Moving from enhancement to transformation*. Workshop at AIS ICT Management and Leadership Conference, Canberra, Australia.

Ratey, J. J., with Hagerman, E. (2008). *Spark: The revolutionary new science of exercise and the brain*. Little, Brown.

Ripley, A. (2021). *High conflict: Why we get trapped and how we get out*. Simon & Schuster.

Robbins, T., & Robbins, S. (Hosts). (2020, November 27). Trading expectations for appreciation [Audio podcast episode]. *The Tony Robbins Podcast*. https://www.tonyrobbins.com/podcasts/trade-expectations-appreciation/

Rowell, L. (2022). *Evolving with gratitude: Small practices in learning communities that make a big difference with kids, peers, and the world.* Impress.

Rubin, G. (2019). *Outer order, inner calm: Declutter and organize to make more room for happiness.* Harmony.

Rumfola, L. M. (2017). *Positive reinforcement positively helps students in the classroom* (Master's thesis). The College at Brockport, State University of New York. https://soar.suny.edu/server/api/core/bitstreams/44286ed4-cd10-442b-b750-664c9c4b3685/content

Santos, L. (Host). (2023, January 2). Stop endlessly chasing the "next big thing" in 2023 [Audio podcast episode]. *The Happiness Lab.* Pushkin Industries. https://www.pushkin.fm/podcasts/the-happiness-lab-with-dr-laurie-santos/stop-endlessly-chasing-the-next-big-thing-in-2023

Selig, M. (2021, August 23). 10 powerful benefits of living with purpose. *Psychology Today.* https://www.psychologytoday.com/us/blog/changepower/202108/10-powerful-benefits-of-living-with-purpose

Seppälä, E., & McNichols, N. K. (2022, June 21). The power of healthy relationships at work. *Harvard Business Review.* https://hbr.org/2022/06/the-power-of-healthy-relationships-at-work

Sinek, S. (2009, September). *How great leaders inspire action* [Video]. TED. https://embed.ted.com/embed/simon_sinek_how_great_leaders_inspire_action

Sinek, S. (2018, October 10). *Love. It's not about intensity, it's about consistency* [Video]. YouTube. https://www.youtube.com/watch?v=6CWbO-GukNw

Tawwab, N. G. (2021). *Set boundaries, find peace: A guide to reclaiming yourself.* TarcherPerigee.

Tawwab, N. G. [@nedratawwab]. (2022, February 4). *Many of us are not practicing self-care. We are practicing after-care* [Instagram reel]. Instagram. https://www.instagram.com/reel/CZj0pjLDc_j/

Terada, Y. (2018, September 11). Welcoming students with a smile. *Edutopia.* https://www.edutopia.org/article/welcoming-students-smile

Tomlinson, C. A. (2017). *How to differentiate instruction in academically diverse classrooms* (3rd ed.). ASCD.

Tricarico, D. (Host). (2021, March 20). 5 questions Zen professionals should ALWAYS be asking [Audio podcast episode]. *The Zen Professional Moment.* https://podcasts.apple.com/us/podcast/5-questions-zen-professionals-should-always-be-asking/id1553865406?i=1000513789854

Urban, M. (2022). *The book of boundaries: Set the limits that will set you free.* The Dial Press.

WCNC.com. (2017, January 31). Teacher connects with students through individualized handshakes. *WCNC.* https://www.wcnc.com/video/news/teacher-connects-with-students-through-individualized-handshakes/275-2495160

Wiens, K. [@kristin.wiens]. (2025, October 4). *When their storm meets our calm, co-regulation occurs* [Illustration]. Instagram. https://www.instagram.com/p/DPZ2jcGj2c1/

Wormeli, R. (2012, July 15). Good feedback is key to active MS learning. *MiddleWeb.* https://www.middleweb.com/1600/ricks-fundamentals-part-2/

Zheng, J., & Meister, M. (2025, January 22). The unbearable slowness of being: Why do we live at 10 bits/s? *Neuron, 113*(2), 192–204.

Index

Note: Page references followed by an italicized *f* indicates information contained in figures.

About the Authors

Suzanne Dailey is a professional developer for the Central Bucks School District in Pennsylvania, where she has the honor and joy of working with more than 500 elementary teachers and 8,000 students across 15 buildings. She teaches model lessons, facilitates professional development sessions, and mentors both new and experienced teachers to be the best they can be for the students in front of them. She has 23 years of teaching experience, primarily in the elementary grades. She taught 4th and 5th grade and served as a reading specialist for kindergarten and 3rd grade. She is National Board–certified and has a master's degree in reading.

Outside teaching, Suzanne is the author of the best-selling ASCD book *Teach Happier This School Year: 40 Weeks of Inspiration and Reflection*. The book walks educators through a typical school year to share small shifts in thought, language, and action that help us professionally and personally. Suzanne is also the host of the popular weekly podcast *Teach Happier*. Short episodes drop on Sundays during the school year to combat the "Sunday Scaries." The goal of each episode is to help listeners get into the healthiest headspace and heartspace possible for their upcoming week of school, whatever their important role may be. You can learn more at www.suzannedailey.com.

Robert Dunlop has been an educator for 23 years. After 12 years in the classroom teaching grades 7 and 8, he took on a central role supporting his district with technology. From there, he became the assessment/evaluation and new teacher consultant supporting a district of 32,000 students across 112 schools. He then spent a short time as a vice principal before going back to the classroom. In 2024, Rob returned to teaching for the first time in 11 years, moving from supporting new teachers across the district to feeling like a new teacher himself.

Robert is the author of *STRIVE for Happiness in Education,* which gives educators a framework for finding more happiness in their profession. He believes that there is nothing more powerful than an educator who loves coming to school every day. He is the co-creator (with a psychologist) of a free staff wellness program tailored for educators that can be found on his website, www.motivatEDU.com. Robert loves to share his message through engaging workshops and speaking engagements.

About ISTE+ASCD

ISTE+ASCD's mission is to empower educators to reimagine and redesign learning through impactful pedagogy and meaningful technology use. We achieve this by offering transformative professional learning, cultivating and disseminating thought leadership, fostering vibrant communities, and ensuring that digital tools and experiences are accessible and effective.

Related Books and Resources

At the time of publication, the following resources related to this book's topic were available:

Building a Strong Foundation: How School Leaders Can Help New Teachers Succeed and Stay, Michelle Hope (Book)

The Classroom of Choice: 100+ Strategies to Reach and Teach Every Learner, 2nd Edition, Jonathan C. Erwin (Book)

Enhancing Professional Practice: The Framework for Teaching, 3rd Edition, Charlotte Danielson, Jim S. Furman, and Lee Kappes (Book)

How to Differentiate Instruction in Academically Diverse Classrooms, 3rd Edition, Carol Ann Tomlinson (Book)

How to Motivate Reluctant Learners, Robyn R. Jackson (Book)

Learning They'll Love: Engage Students, Meet Standards, and Spark Creativity with Personal Interest Projects, Elizabeth Agro Radday (Book)

The New Teacher's Companion: Practical Wisdom for Succeeding in the Classroom, Gini Cunningham (Book)

Small but Mighty: How Everyday Habits Add Up to More Manageable and Confident Teaching, Miriam Plotinsky (Book)

Smart from the Start: 100 Tools for Teaching with Confidence, James H. Stronge, Jessica M. Straessle, and Xianxuan Xu (Book)

Teach for Authentic Engagement, Lauren Porosoff (Book)

Teach Happier This School Year: 40 Weeks of Inspiration and Reflection, Suzanne Dailey (Book)

For up-to-date information about ISTE+ASCD books and resources, go to www.iste-ascd.org/books. To learn more about membership and join or renew, go to iste-ascd.org/membership, email memsupport@iste-ascd.org, or call 1-800-933-2723 or 703-578-9600.